Leading Through
Relationship
First

**Building a Great Team Through a
Commitment to Servant Leadership**

Henry Jordan

Printing History
Edition One, April 2015

ISBN: 978-1-943070-00-8

Leading Through Relationship First:
Building a Great Team Through a
Commitment to Servant Leadership

Dedication

The contribution of so many people must be recognized in the writing of this book. From my initial meeting with Sam Walton, the great people I worked with and for, my apostle F. Nolan Ball and his wife Shirley, my family, friends, and my faith, all are a significant part of the leadership style I possess today. Most of all, my wife and best friend for the past 30 years, Caroline, you are my sunshine and the biggest contributor to this work and the man I have become.

My motivation and dedication in writing this book is to emphasize and remind every person in a leadership role – the people on the front line – they are the ones with the greatest potential to make an impact. I hope to inspire great servant leaders to bring out the best in all of us.

Preface

In this book, I share what I have learned over the past 30 years of working with great people from around the country as I moved up the ranks from hourly employee, to mid-level manager, to senior vice president. As a young man at the age of 21, I had my first encounter with Sam Walton, the founder of Walmart. This encounter impacted my life and career and inspired a leadership style based on servant leadership with relationship as the core foundation.

Great leaders like Sam Walton and Walt Disney understood the need for servant leadership. Their success was the result, in large part, of their willingness and ability to relate to their people and their people to them. While both of these legendary leaders had a dream, it was only through people that their dreams became a reality. When those in charge are willing to put forth the effort to build quality relationships with people, these leaders are demonstrating servant leadership. Servant leadership is the act of considering others before yourself, demonstrating you care, and making decisions in the best interest of the people and the company. In this type of environment, the people are more informed and willing to trust the decisions that are made, and will be committed to the purpose and vision of the organization.

There is a great need for teaching servant leadership in the organizational environment today. It is my hope that you will use this book as a tool to build a great team, while realizing it can only be accomplished through your commitment to serving those whom you lead.

What people have said about

Henry Jordan's
Leadership

"Thank you for your leadership and support. The learning experience I gained while touring with you has helped me to develop not only personally, but to develop my team as well. You have honestly given me a true passion for whom I want to become and how I would like to develop my career."

Kori, *Store Manager*

"You have always been the person who speaks up for those who lost their voices and have served as a compass for so many that have lost their way."

Jeffery, *Divisional Human Resource Leader*

"You are one of the very best at what you do. I always admired your style, your substance, your collaborative approach, and your personal touch with people."

Mark, *Vice President of Merchandising*

"Your mentorship and support truly made an impact on my career that continues to guide me today. Your passion for the business and taking care of people continues to be something I strive to emulate in my leadership role."

Jim, *Market Manager*

"You have motivated me and my market manager to really think outside of the box for my operation and really take our results to the next level."

Brian, *Store Manager*

"Your professionalism along with your respect for the individual has always been so impressive."

Teri, *Divisional Replenishment Manager*

What people have said about

Henry Jordan's
Leadership

"You have impacted my career greatly. I will always remember your emphasis on family and the stories about your Jack Russell Terrier. I will strive to be a servant leader that helps and impacts others as you have impacted me."

Rudy, *Store Manager*

"The things you shared with me, both constructive and challenging, I have respected, shared with others, and will never forget. I will always respect your leadership and teachings."

Michelle, *Store Manager*

"I will always remember you as an individual with integrity and passion, and one who fulfills the commitments he makes."

Abdul, *Divisional Health & Wellness Director*

"I've personally always been impressed with the respectful way that you work with others and the level of excellence that you have delivered in everything that you have done."

Brian, *Senior Director Health & Wellness*

"You are a great leader, a brilliant retailer, a fantastic motivator, and someone that people want to follow."

Patrick, *Director of Communications*

"You are one of those leaders I could always count on for your values and in your approach."

Paul, *Senior Vice President of Health & Wellness*

Table of

Contents

Relationship First will help you to benefit from the experience of others and their mistakes while becoming the type of leader people will want to follow.

Introduction

Millions of hard working people wake up every morning with a desire to accomplish something great. Millions of managers and leaders wake up every day and desire the same. This book is designed as a tool to help you gain a better understanding of how to bring out the best in your people and in yourself and how to fuse these two desires into one. As we walk through five seasons of building a great team, my hope is for you to reflect on your personal approach to leadership and to allow me to challenge you to become a person of significant influence – a genuine leader that can truly inspire greatness from the people around you. I want to challenge you to become an effective leader that delivers results the right way – through establishing *Relationship First* with your people. Life is a great teacher. Through mistakes and successes over time, most people eventually figure out how to make progress toward the goals set before them. The problem is that this takes time, and mistakes can be costly. *Relationship First* will help you to benefit from the experience of others and their mistakes while becoming the type of leader people will want to follow.

Throughout my personal career, every assignment that I was given had one thing in common: I was responsible for building a team and leading that team to success. If you are reading this book, it is likely that this challenge is also facing you on a daily basis. While the geographic element of the assignments I was given may have varied along with the scope and scale of the same, these common questions were always present – how do I build a great team, inspire team members to be committed to a common vision or goal, and achieve great results for the organization?

There are many authors and great leadership experts out there today who can provide all types of great insights on leading a team more effectively. The challenge is that you first have to build a team before you can lead it. In the following pages we will walk through five phases I have found to be critical in order to build a great team and to become a successful servant leader of people.

We will first talk about the importance of relationship or the ability to relate to your people and your people to you. Relationship is the only bridge that can connect the ability and potential of hard working people with the vision and purpose of a leader. Relationship is the only bridge that can connect desire and experience with passion and success. Relationship is the only bridge that can connect the effort of an individual with the momentum of a team. It is only through relationship that leaders can connect with the people they are given the opportunity to lead. Relationship is the reinforced foundation that will enable you to build a great team, a team that is committed to you and to the organization.

Next, we take a look at the nature of expectations and why they are so important. Does every member of your team understand the role he or she plays in the overall team's success? Does every player have a clear vision of what is expected of him or her? Most importantly, does everyone on your team have the same understanding of what "good" looks like? We will discuss a few simple exercises you can utilize to measure your team's current engagement level and perception.

The third chapter builds upon the first two and walks through the process of alignment providing great tips for gaining continuity in the expectations you have established across your organization. When people align together behind a common goal, the team begins to experience momentum and leverage. Strengths are joined to strengths, and movement is the result.

The fourth chapter is the most challenging for leaders – adjustment. This chapter discusses the realization that a leader often will be faced with a team that is not performing to its full potential due to having the wrong people in the wrong place. Be sure to put on your managerial courage hat before reading this chapter, as you will be challenged to sometimes make changes that are not easy but are critical for the overall team's success.

The fifth chapter is the capstone – fine-tuning. Not many teams make it to this point of maturity, but for those that do, good things happen for all involved. Fine-tuning is going from good to great, from a conference championship to winning the super bowl. It is about running faster, jumping higher, and closing the gaps on the little things that can continue to add momentum and efficiency.

Now, given the lack of patience that most of us possess today, it is tempting to go straight to Chapter 5 and think you are ready to fine-tune your team. Keep in mind that you have to build an engine before you can tune it! Read the first four chapters. They establish the foundation that every great team must have. If you are willing to examine your current leadership style and think about your people from a different perspective, you can take your team to the next level. Throughout my 30-year career, I have had the privilege of leading several great teams through this exciting phase of fine-tuning, and let me tell you – it is worth the extra effort!

The sixth chapter describes what happens if a leader ignores the first five chapters of the book. It is called the "Perils of Micromanaging." We have all likely worked in an environment at some point in our careers where we were micromanaged. There are many frustrations that come from this poor style of managing people, and we discuss the consequences, both short term and long term, and how to get back on track if you find yourself being this type of leader.

I hope you enjoy reading *Relationship First* as much as I enjoyed writing it. This overall approach to building a highly impactful and successful team is a compilation of what all the great people I have worked with in the past 30 years have taught me about what it truly takes to become a great leader. Building a team through the establishment of a strong foundation first will ensure you build a legacy that remains for a long time. Relationship is the foundation of the supervisor-employee arrangement. When you as a leader take the time to understand the needs of your people, they will respond with great cooperation, commitment, and respect. I dare you to try it. I encourage you on your journey to becoming the type of leader that people will make the personal choice to follow. Enjoy!

Chapter 1

Relationship

When it comes to the topic of relationship, the first one that comes to mind is a relationship with a husband or wife or maybe kids, and rightfully so. We work hard to provide and care for these people every day. Beyond immediate family, there are other family relationships and relationships with our friends. These are also important as our lives are filled with memories made spending time with those we care about. Spiritual relationships are also at the top of mind for many people and help them to find purpose, guidance, and a sense of belonging and peace.

The other realm of relationship is the one that this book is written about, the role of relationships in our occupations and with the people we lead. Whether you are a coach of a little league team of 10-year-olds, a college football coach, a CEO of a Fortune 100 company, or a shift supervisor at a coffee shop, your success is dependent upon the success of your people. Your people want you to help them accomplish great things. They want to know that you care about them. Whether you win or lose, and often times whether they win or lose, is dependent upon the environment and relationship that you as the leader establish with them.

When it comes to these relationships in our occupations, this realm of relationship seldom receives the amount of attention from the leader that it deserves. If you will take the time to understand the importance of and how to establish a strong foundation of *Relationship First* with the people you lead, you will be amazed at the level of success that you, with your team, can accomplish.

How do you define the word relationship? Most people would think of the romantic element first, then the family, and then the others. For the sake of this discussion, I would like to reference the definition by Merriam-Webster that defines relationship as "the state of being related or interrelated, a state of affairs existing between those having relations or dealings." In other words, relationship requires that people be able to relate to one another. Have you ever worked for someone you just could not relate to? Have you ever worked for someone you could relate to? What was the difference? Do you see yourself as a leader people can relate to? What determines if people can or cannot relate to someone in leadership and vice versa? Why does it matter? It is actually pretty simple. If you want to relate to the people you lead, you should first find common ground with them. What do you have in common with them? There are always areas of common interest if one is willing to put a small amount of effort toward finding them.

Let me give you an example. Harry gets promoted to regional manager and takes a training trip with his mentor.

They travel to one of the company's facilities, and Harry's mentor assembles a group of about 100 employees for Harry to speak to. Harry greets the group and immediately begins trying to impress everyone with his new title and comments about the business. After about five minutes, it is obvious to his mentor that Harry has completely lost the group's attention. People are looking at their phones and watches and are completely disengaged. Harry's mentor steps in and says, "Let me ask everyone a question. Who in this room has the biggest dog at home?" Everyone immediately smiled, laughed and became instantly engaged in the conversation. For the next 15 minutes, Harry's mentor led the discussion about dogs – big and small, old and young, obedient and full of trouble. Harry also participated and talked about his Labrador retriever. After the "dog" discussion, Harry started over with the group and led a very engaged discussion around the business. Later that evening, Harry shared with his mentor the valuable lessons he learned that day. If people know you first as a person, as an individual, as a normal guy with a dog, they will then seek to know you as a leader. Starting out with the "look what I know" approach is never a good idea. Titles? Take your title and bit of luck, and you might be able to buy a cheap cup of coffee. Be humble. Great leaders know they are promoted to serve, not to be served.

The art of building relationships should be viewed from a wide perspective. Some relationships are very short term and must be established quickly, while others can take time and a slower-paced approach. In the case of Harry, he was challenged with establishing a common ground with his audience within a few minutes so that he could effectively communicate with them through his comments on the business. Dynamic speakers will often develop this ability as it is critical in order for them to hold their audiences' attention. To bring this back to the workplace, most of us are challenged with building relationships with groups of people whom we have opportunities to work with every day and can take a more thought-out, longer-term approach. Most job assignments last from one to three or four years giving you a great opportunity to get to know your people. The important point here is to realize that you can always find common ground with people if you are willing to put forth the effort. Relating is a two-way street. When you realize that you have found that common place with them, they will usually have done the same with you.

When a leader understands the importance of establishing relationships first with his or her people, the leader begins to set the stage for something great to happen. In too many cases, hard-working people show up at their places of employment, do their jobs, and go home. These types of transactional relationships between people and their employers are way too common. People comply with the "rules" set forth by the upper leadership of the company, most of whom they do not know or have never even met. Too many leaders are focused not on their people but on themselves and their personal ambitions. Too many leaders use their positions, their titles, or their credentials alone to try and earn the respect of their people. It does not work. People will comply because they have to. People commit because they want to.

So how does a leader tap into this critical foundation called relationship to establish a truly effective team? Check your ego. Be a great servant leader to your people. Carefully consider how your decisions and those of your organization will affect the people you lead. Very simply put – don't be a jerk. Next time you are with a group of colleagues, ask them about the best and worst leaders they have ever worked for. Ask them what made the difference between the two and how they felt about working for that person. What you will find is a clear distinction between having a job versus having a future, having a task versus a purpose, having a relationship of trust as opposed to never knowing what will happen next.

Successful leaders understand that in order to achieve maximum results, they must ensure they understand the strengths and weaknesses of each player or employee in order to ensure each person is put in the role where they can leverage their strengths and provide maximum contribution to the overall team. Don't overthink the act of relating to your people. Internalize the challenge and think about someone you trust and respect. What has that person done to make you feel that way? Was it a kind act, a personal hand-written note, a heart-felt speech in a meeting, or maybe a glimpse of who that person is as an individual versus a person with a title? Remember that anyone can relate to a nice guy who loves his dog or a lady who is proud of her kids. This is the relationship side of life; take time to let people see this side of you, and they will begin to relate to who you are.

Sam Walton, the founder of Walmart, knew relationship was important. He knew that it was important to know your people and let them know you. Early in my career, I heard Mr. Sam say in a corporate meeting, "Success happens when you get the right people in the right place at the right time." Have you ever worked in an environment or played on a team where it was obvious that people were in the wrong positions? This can occur for many reasons but seldom has a happy ending. A friend of mine has a son who played high school football. The son was a tight end and was obviously dependent on the quarterback to throw a catchable pass in order for him to contribute to the team. The young man at the quarterback position was not a very good passer, and the other parents on the team began to pressure the coach to make a change. The coach eventually admitted to one of the parents that the quarterback was the son of a major contributor to the sports program, which was the reason for him staying in the quarterback position.

We have all observed someone being in a position where he or she did not fit. It creates a great deal of frustration for everyone else and limits the overall team's ability to succeed. Allowing this situation to go on for an extended period of time will also cause others to lose respect and trust for the leader who allows it to happen without responding. The football team had some success but never won a major championship. Good leaders and good coaches will work through the local politics to ensure that the right people are in the right place and that they are put there at the right time. There is no other way to build a true championship team in business or in sports.

So let's talk about trust. In *Leadership: Theory and Practice*, Peter Northouse wrote, "People want to have a trusting relationship with their leaders. In exchange, people are willing to give leaders greater loyalty and commitment." Loyalty and commitment – two critical elements for effective teams that are found only where trust exists in the relationship. I have never met a leader who did not agree that trust was a critical component of building a great team. So let's consider where trust comes from. Think about this: People will only trust someone they understand, and to understand a person you must have some means of relating to them. Another way to view this point is to realize that trust can only be developed through relationship. Let me give you an example. Joe goes to work one day and learns that his supervisor has been promoted and a new one has been assigned to his area. Like most of us would, Joe seeks to learn from his peers and from the new supervisor's bio anything he can about his new boss. While Joe has heard a few things about the new leader, he looks forward to the time when he can hear from her personally. Within the a few days, Joe gets a call to have a one-on-one meeting with his new boss. During the meeting, she asks Joe all about his family, his experience, what he is passionate about in life, and his personal goals within the organization. She also takes time to share the same with him. This is really important. People want to know more about you as a person than they do about you as the vice president or director. If you focus on letting them see you as a person first, then as their leader, it will really help people relate to you. Don't make the mistake of hiding behind your name badge. It never creates trust with your people. In fact, often times when you assume a new role with a new group of people, you also are assuming the perspective and opinion the people have of the last person in that role. That perception may or may not be a good one. So let's go back to Joe. During the meeting, his new boss says all the right things, and he feels really positive about the first impression. Over the next few weeks and months, Joe continues to grow in his respect for her as she always speaks to him in the hall, asks his opinion in meetings, and never forgets to ask how his kids are doing. Joe even receives a hand-written note from her commending him for having the highest sales week among his peers.

Now many of you at this point may be asking, "What is a hand-written note?" I know. We are all addicted to texting and emailing today, but once in a while write a note to someone to say thanks or good job. It will be good for you and *great* for them. I have been in the business environment for over 30 years, and I believe I still have almost every note I ever received from one of my superiors. When your people know that you recognize their individual contributions, it again is an avenue to build trust. If I work hard, someone will notice. If employees enjoy the work they do and feel appreciated, they are more likely to stay engaged and be more committed to the company. When people know that their leadership and the company they work for are willing to invest in their future, it increases the level of employee engagement and commitment to the overall vision and mission of the business. Most importantly, if people know someone cares about their future, they will in turn pass this caring on to the customer.

If Joe's new boss continues this approach with him, which could be simply defined as establishing relationship, trust will eventually become a product of his new boss's efforts. Joe will then wake up every day committed to helping his team accomplish something great, as opposed to just complying with the rules and putting in his eight hours a day for a paycheck. As summarized by Richard Conlow in *Excellence in Supervision*, relationship establishes a connection with people, expectation ensures they are clear as to what they are being asked to do, and motivation gives them the encouragement and desire to ensure a strong commitment to success.

I believe that appreciation and recognition are among the most under-utilized resources available to leaders and managers today. When people are corrected or punished, they spend the next element of time trying their best to forget that it happened. When people are recognized and appreciated, they seem to never forget, and they never stop talking about it. Taking the time to acknowledge the contributions of the individuals on your staff will go a long way in establishing and maintaining strong relationships with them. Recognition typically costs very little, yet it is invaluable to the person on the other end. I began using hand-written note cards very early in my career, and I never stopped. My wife, Caroline, would make them on our home computer when I was a young store manager, before they were available elsewhere. Why? It's pretty simple; I remember how good it felt when someone took a moment to appreciate my efforts. I wanted to always be a leader who was known for appreciating the people around me. It feels really good to make someone's day with a simple note card in the mail. Some of the responses I received were pretty amazing. I remember receiving a thank you card in the mail a few years ago. At first, I did not recognize the name on the return address. Upon opening the card, I read the following: "I would like to thank you so much for the note you sent me. I have been in the retail business for over 35 years and never had someone send me a hand-written note. I showed most of the associates in my facility." Wow – it was a thank you note for sending a thank you note. That is pretty amazing. On another occasion, I conducted a store visit, and the facility looked great. The manager gave a great deal of credit to his overnight crew – many of whom I had never met. I had him bring a piece of poster board, and I wrote a big thank you note for him to post by the time clock. The poster board cost less than $3 and took me two minutes to write. A few weeks later I received a package in the mail with a t-shirt with the store number on the front and a blown up copy of my note on the back! My first thought was, "Did I spell everything right?" Thank goodness I did. My point is that these little gestures of appreciation are worth their weight in gold to the people on the receiving end. Never withhold appreciation and recognition from those around you. It is a powerful motivational tool that will help your people to relate to you, trust you, and be committed to do what you are asking them to do. How many associates in your area of responsibility have never received a gesture of appreciation? The answer might surprise you.

As one considers why recognition and appreciation are so powerful, it really comes down to the person on the receiving end knowing that you are looking out for his or her best interest. As I said earlier, it builds trust when someone knows that you recognize his or her contributions. We have all worked for people who simply do not have it in their DNA to say thank you. The reason most leaders state for this behavior is that they do not want to let up driving results. That makes about as much sense as not stopping to put gas in your car for fear of wasting time. Sorry – this is a very shallow approach to leadership and one that simply does not work. For those leaders, I have some advice: Stop making deposits in your checking account but continue writing checks. See how that works out for you. Sam Walton was a master at making people feel important and valued. I have two letters that he sent to me in the late 1980s. Both letters were personally signed, and I still have them framed today. In his memoir *Sam Walton: Made In America*, Mr. Sam stated, "There is no substitute for being honest with someone and letting them know they didn't do a good job. But there's no better way to keep someone doing things the right way than by letting him or her know how much you appreciate their performance. If you do that one simple thing, human nature will take it from there."

As I reflect back on the people who impacted my life and career, it is interesting to see what those individuals all had in common. They were not perfect, and they knew that. They all worked hard and had great passion for what they did. They were all very intelligent and great businesspeople. While all of these attributes were a factor in their success, the most significant thing about these people was their humble approach to leadership, their integrity, and their ability to appreciate, motivate, and encourage others. If you take the time to examine those leaders that have impacted you over the years, I bet you will find similar traits. The truth is that this type of investment in others is what motivates people and causes them to go above and beyond what is required. As stated so well by Stephen Young in his 2007 book, *Micro Messaging: Why Great Leadership is Beyond Words*, "Labels of authority have nothing to do with whether others consider you a leader or whether they'd be motivated to follow you." It really is pretty simple when you think about it in this way. If you think about struggling leaders or smart people who have been short lived in their success, they also have some things in common. They seldom take the time to build relationships with their people, other than a select few for show. They operate in an environment of compliance versus commitment because that is the extent of the response they can get from their people. This type of leader expects everyone to comply with his or her wishes without question. The outcome is a transactional situation where no ownership, trust, or conviction is present among the people. We look again to Peter Northouse who stated, "In contrast to transactional leadership, transformational leadership is the process whereby a person engages with others and creates a connection that raises the level of motivation and morality in both the leader and the follower. This type of leader is attentive to the needs and motives of followers and tries to help followers reach their fullest potential."

As leaders in any arena, we must establish relationship and trust with our people. When trust is not present between a leader and the people he or she is seeking to lead, very little can be accomplished. Again in his memoir Mr. Sam said, "What has carried this company so far so fast is the relationship that we, the managers, have been able to enjoy with our associates." If Mr. Sam were still with us today, one can bet that he would still be emphasizing the relationship he valued with the people he worked with. Sam seemed to know that taking the time to maintain good relationships and a sense of trust with the people would ensure they, in turn, took great care of his customers. When a lack of trust exists in an organization, it has a way of cascading all the way through each level of the infrastructure until it ultimately affects the customer on the front line. People in this type of environment become hesitant to make decisions, suppressed in their ability to think creatively and often become frustrated to the point of seeking a way to a better future.

There are many issues and behaviors that can lead to an erosion of trust among leaders and followers. Good leaders must demonstrate effective listening skills, patience and open-mindedness, and be willing to show they care on a frequent basis. Don Soderquist, another leader who is well known for his cultural influence on Walmart, wrote in his book *The Wal-Mart Way: The Inside Story of the Success of the World's Largest Company*, "When you create win-win relationships with your business partnerships based on trust and open communications, you maximize your potential for growth." If all you want to do is to create an environment of compliance where people come and go for a paycheck, then never say thank you. If you want to establish a firm foundation of relationship and trust that you can build a championship team upon, use appreciation and recognition often. It will amaze you how effective it can be.

Speaking of a championship team, at the end of the day, that is what all leaders are trying to build. Think about this – what do a fifth grade football coach, a shift manager at a coffee shop, a general manager of a commercial bakery, and a CEO of a multi-billion dollar company all have in common? Their success is totally dependent upon their ability to put the right people in the right place on the team and to motivate team members to give their best effort. What role does relationship play in this process? It is critical. Through taking the time to relate to your people as individuals first, you can then understand what role on the team they can most effectively fulfill. Many leaders allow the size of their responsibility to serve as an excuse for not attempting to relate to the people they lead. That is a mistake. Regardless of the size of your organization, you can find ways to let people see your heart. In the example of the poster board note left for the overnight crew in that particular facility, I was able to establish a connection with over 40 people just through a simple gesture. Then, as hundreds of other employees observed the note, they too were impacted and immediately developed a perception of my leadership. Think about your venues of communication. Whether in weekly meetings, annual corporate gathering speeches, or something out of the ordinary that you choose to do for a small group that goes viral in the organization, you can relate to and inspire your people if you just apply effort toward doing so.

Relating to your people is also important so that you can understand what makes them tick and understand the skillsets and attributes they bring to the table. It takes much longer to deal with a bad decision than it takes to make a good one in the beginning. We have all made this mistake. We get in a hurry and fill an important job with someone we hope is the right fit only to spend the next year dealing with the consequences of that poor decision. Spend time with your people. Figure out what they are good at, what they love to do, where their passions lie, and what they have that can fuse together with the other talents on your team. If you want to build a great team, you must ensure your people can complement one another with their talents. Jerry Rice and Joe Montana were, by many accounts, two of the greatest football players to ever play for the NFL. During their years together playing for the San Francisco 49ers, they were unstoppable. Montana had the arm to throw incredible passes, and Rice had the hands to catch them. Together, they accomplished many victories. What do you suppose would have happened if the coach had these two reversed? Would they have been as successful if Montana had been placed as a wide receiver and Rice had been put in the position of quarterback? Not likely. In football, the coaches do their homework. They take the time to understand every player, inside and out. They seek to understand every expertise, ability, attitude, and thought process of each of their players individually, so when the players get on the field, they can function as a team. Coaches watch how the players run and how they move, observe their attitudes and abilities, and seek to understand how they think. Now think about this scenario in the workplace. How many times have we all observed a wide receiver trying to function as a quarterback? The collateral damage can be high, and there is seldom a happy ending.

Just a few years ago, I had the opportunity to spend an afternoon with a well-known and very successful college football coach. The coach took me into the conference room where he and his assistant coaches met daily to have team meetings. On one side of the room the entire wall was filled with several large chalkboards. Written on the chalkboards were hundreds of names of up-and-coming high school kids from around the country. Coach explained how important it was to understand where his players are from, what makes them tick, where their strengths and weaknesses lie, and what kind of families they came from. He explained the importance of getting to know the players on the team individually in order to build a team that had championship potential. I have met this coach on several different occasions, each time seeing him with one of the players, talking, listening, and fostering the relationship between the two of them. Now think about this scenario in the workplace. Think about the individuals on your team today. Are you confident that each person is in his or her right place? Do their results confirm that they are? Take time to learn what makes your people who they are. Talk to them, listen to them, and find out what makes them tick. Build a relationship with them that can help you to put them in an environment where they can be their best.

When I talk about building relationships, I am not talking about fraternization. I am not talking about friendships. There are many opportunities in the proper working environment for leaders to get to know their people. Look for these opportunities and capitalize on them. An occasional trip offsite with your team to enjoy a cross-country hike or visit a museum can provide a great opportunity to further your relationship in a different setting. Remember – the right people, right place and right time equal a winning team.

When people know that their leadership and the company they work for are willing to invest in their future, it increases the level of employee engagement and commitment to the overall vision and mission of the business. Most importantly, if people know someone cares about their future, they will in turn pass this caring on to the customer.

Chapter One
Reflections

- How well do you really know your core team members? Should you spend more time understanding their passions, skills, qualifications, and future ambitions?

- Are you taking the time to talk to your people in group settings, staff meetings, corporate meetings, and other gatherings where you can help them to know you better?

- When you consider the perception you have developed with each team member, is this based primarily on assumption and on what others have told you, or is it the result of one-on-one time you have spent conversing with him or her personally?

- Can your people relate to you on a level that produces trust? How often do they disagree with you or share a conflicting opinion knowing you will listen?

- Are you a good listener who gives your team your undivided attention, so you can absorb the message people are trying to send to you? Or do you commonly do most of the talking?

- How much time do you spend each week on venues of appreciation? How far reaching are your efforts? Are your venues personal enough in nature? (If Mr. Sam had time to send personal notes, you really have no excuse.)
- Is the work environment you create one of commitment or compliance?
- When you think about the best and worst leaders you have worked for, which one do you most resemble?
- As you consider your current team members, how confident are you that you have the right people in the right place?
- How are your overall results? How do these results compare to the quality and current state of your team? If you are happy with your results, is the current trend sustainable or short-lived?
- What changes do you feel need to be made in your leadership style in order to ensure you have a firm foundation of relationship to build your team upon? Are you willing to make those changes?
- When is the last time you took your team on a field trip outside of work to explore a museum or hiking trail?

... if you want to build a highly productive and engaged team of people around you, you have to take the time to let them know the expectation, let them know why it is important, discuss with them the best alternatives available to attain the desired results, and make them participants (not just an audience) in the entire process.

Chapter 2

Expectations

Expectations – what are they and why are they so important? When an individual joins a company and takes on a new job, he or she comes to the job with clear expectations on what to expect from an employer: an agreed upon pay rate, a reasonable work schedule, fair and equitable treatment from management and their co-workers, and the opportunity for a successful career path, just to name a few. A great deal of effort is put into making sure that the employee's expectations are transparent and understood by both parties. Most companies do a nice job of clarifying the general guidelines to live by within the organization, covering rules and laws related to compliance, wage and hour regulations, etc. But expectations of the employees in their jobs or roles are not quite as clear. Many managers take the approach to place the person in the new job, tell them the broad parameters to abide within, and send them into battle with a nice pat on the back saying,

"Make it happen!" The problem is we often do not clarify well enough what "it" really means. In these situations, people begin to interpret on their own what they should be doing and how they should be doing it. Some people will be great on their own, some will be average, and some will do as little as possible to get by in these situations. Even the people doing as little as possible are typically not poor workers; they just lack expectations. If you have ever walked into a place of business that was extremely unorganized and where everyone seemed to be doing his or her own thing, it is likely that expectations are exactly the problem. Just to be clear, I am not saying this situation is the fault of the employee or that the average employee does not want to do the right thing. On the contrary, I believe most people want to do well, be successful in their jobs and please their employers. The problem typically lies with the manager or leader who fails to define clearly what good looks like.

Great leaders learn to answer questions before they are asked, thereby avoiding the possible negative experience the customer can encounter due to a lack of preparation or training. If a company fails to take the time to instill clear expectations for their people on an ongoing basis, the level of productivity and customer experience can suffer. The establishment of clear expectations is one of the most effective leadership actions, yet it is one of the most underutilized. Conlow wrote, "All good performance begins with clear expectations and goals." Expectations are necessary for everyone within an organization, from those responsible for the simplest task to the officers of the company and at every level in between. As a leader, you must give people a road map of simple expectations to understand where they are, where you want them to go, and how to get there. By constantly re-enforcing the expectations and goals, everyone is more likely to stay focused on the right priorities and work collaboratively together to see them achieved.

It is rare to see a situation where the goals or expectations create conflict. More often, it is the manner in which these expectations are communicated or the means by which people are allowed to pursue different venues of achieving these expectations that causes conflict. Many large organizations today have replaced creative imagination and new idea generation from the field with a small group of innovations managers in the home office. The best organizations will make provisions for both. Corporations must gather raw ideas and input from the people on the front line and use this valuable source of information to feed the activity of the innovations team. By establishing clear expectations and goals and then providing a high degree of flexibility on how to achieve the goals, organizations can realize a greater level of success.

When it comes to communicating expectations, the higher a position in a company, the more emphasis should be placed on the expected outcome versus *how* the individual must achieve the results. At lower levels in the organization, however, great detail can and should be provided regarding productivity levels, operational standards, how to handle and treat customers, and how to approach issues regarding compliance and laws that govern the business venue. Let me encourage you not to make setting the expectations a one-sided conversation. Let me also encourage you to keep it real. Most people have worked in an environment at some point in their careers where the expectations were so high that they were impossible to attain. Leaders often use this approach as a means of getting their people to reach for the very best results possible, all the while frustrating their teams. What would it be like for a football team if the objective was to score a touchdown but the goal line continually moved away as the team approached it? Eventually, they would stop trying. People in the business environment are no different. Goals and expectations can be very high and attainable at the same time. That is why people are in leadership roles, to lead their teams with balanced, well-thought-out expectations.

While some companies will try to set expectations by having a new employee sit alone in front of a computer module for days, the more effective companies will conduct the orientation and expectation session face to face with the person or group of people being oriented. The interpretation of what *good* looks like should involve the associate or person you are dealing with. On occasion, their ideas will build upon what you may have set as the current standard or process. Even on the simple tasks, you want the associate involved to take ownership from day one. Ask questions during the process of setting expectations. Tell your team why certain things are important and allow team members to help build upon the process.

Sam Walton was passionate about surfacing input from his associates. In fact, during the early years of Walmart, there were numerous programs in place for hourly associates to send in new ideas to the home office. Many of the practices in place at the company today are the result of an associate sending an idea to someone at the home office who later adopted it. On a few occasions as a young store manager, I sent a few ideas to Mr. Sam personally. He acknowledged each idea with a personal letter back to me. One of the ideas I submitted was to hand out smiley stickers at the front door to children entering our store. We had tested this locally with huge success, and he listened to the idea. A few months later, it became a company-wide program. In the years that followed, the smiley face became the marketing icon for the company. My point? Many ideas are out there if you are willing to create an opportunity for them to be heard.

As you consider new people joining the company or joining your team, always do your best to establish ownership on the part of every associate from the very beginning, so each person knows that what he does matters. You want people to come into the company with the encouragement to share their fresh perspective of the way things are done. Often when visiting with the newest people in my areas of responsibility, I would ask them to share their perspectives of the company and their jobs. The feedback was always insightful, fresh, and valuable.

I spent many of my early years in retail doing whatever jobs and tasks in the operation needed to be done. I have pulled shopping carts, cleaned bathrooms, and stocked shelves along the way. What is interesting is who taught me the right way to do these jobs. It was seldom a supervisor or other leader of the company; it was always a great associate who had been taught what *good* looked like. Involve your people at every level in helping your team to establish the individual expectations for each position on the team. Be proactive in setting and agreeing on what the expectations are and keep them involved. They are waiting on you to ask for their help. The associates are the ones that you really depend on to make your team's success a reality.

While there is an opportunity to produce great results through clear, aligned expectations, there is also a great risk that exists in any organization when expectation's are not clear. According to Patrick Montana and Bruce Charnov in their 2008 book *Management*, "If you do not take the initiative to clearly define what you expect, do not think that your employees will not make their own assumptions, leaving both sides wide open for frustration and disappointment later." Talk to your team about what you need from it. Let team members know what is expected and discuss the different venues available to produce the desired result. When a group of people look at an objective and the most efficient manner to achieve success, the quality and depth of evaluating the possibilities is much higher than when this process is left up to the interpretation of just one. When leaders involve their people in determining the best possible course or solution to achieve the desired result, it gives the people involved a sense of ownership in the process. When I understand what you want me to do and you involve me in the discussion of how we can get there, I feel engaged, appreciated, and empowered to exceed the expectation at hand. As stated so well by Adrian Gostick and Chester Elton in their popular book *The Carrot Principle*, "While leaders cannot often change the tasks in their organizations, they can change employees' attitudes toward their jobs by setting clear corporate or team goals. By defining the purpose of a task and tying it to a desirable end result, effective leaders infuse work with meaning and purpose." Remember – if you want to build a highly productive and engaged team of people around you, you have to take the time to let them know the expectation, let them know why it is important, discuss with them the best alternatives available to attain the desired results, and make them participants (not just an audience) in the entire process. This investment will cause your people to be committed to a purpose, not just compliant with a job.

Many of you may have participated in group exercises that seek to demonstrate the power of expectations. I remember participating in a management development course on one occasion where our table of six people was asked to perform a simple task. A jar of marbles was poured onto the floor. We were asked to get up and place the marbles back into the jar. We casually got up from our chairs and did what was asked, and it took about a minute. After taking our seats once again, the leader poured the marbles back onto the floor and this time asked us to place the marbles back into the jar within 30 seconds. The entire mode of our team changed. We immediately got up from our chairs, strategically got in position in a circle around the marbles, and waited on the leader to say GO! While this example is extremely simple in nature, it points out the importance of the manner in which we as leaders choose to set expectations of others on our team. The interesting thing that happened in this scenario is that we did the same task in half the time. We were more thoughtful and were very proud that we had achieved the task set before us in less than the 30 seconds given. Think about your organization and the expectations you have set regarding productivity, attitude, customer service, and operational standards. Does your team know what good looks like? If it does, you are well on your way to helping them achieve it. If not, take the time to show them what is good and why. You will see immediate results. Keep this in mind: If your people do not learn what *good* looks like and how to achieve it on a consistent basis, they will never be able to deliver *great*.

Early in my career, I had a small, high-volume store in my area of responsibility. Because the store was small, there were a limited number of employees that worked at the facility. In order for the facility to provide a great shopping experience for the customers, it took everyone in the store working cross-functionally together to achieve success. When I visited the store and asked the employees why they were not chipping in and helping one another, the answer was simple. They stated, "No one has ever ask us to do so." We asked, they responded, and the store began working as a team and quickly became a huge success. While not all problems in the workplace can be resolved so easily, many can be if the leadership will ensure expectations are made clear.

Expectations should be accompanied with explanations as well. While it was a good exercise to make a point, if the people at our table were asked to pick up marbles every day for a week, at some point we are going to want to know why our task is so important. Take the time to explain to your team members *why* you want them to do *what* you are asking of them. When people truly understand how their jobs tie to the greater purpose of the organization, they are more likely to respond with a commitment to you and to the roles they play. If they are just told every day to come in and pick up marbles, they are likely to respond with varying levels of compliance and only as part of a transactional relationship with you and the company. "I do this job – I get a paycheck" is not very exciting or sustainable. People have an inherent need to be a part of something good, to know that what they do matters to the overall effort and organization. Give your team clear expectations at every level, and you will begin to see immediate improvement in your results.

Measurement is a core part of setting clear expectations. Often an expectation is set in a given situation but never followed up on or measured to see how the individual or particular team is performing. Human beings seem to be naturally competitive. Even the most reserved person on your team will typically have a competitive vein if you are willing to look for it. During my years as an officer at Walmart, I always enjoyed playing a major role in the company's annual fund raising campaign for children's hospitals. The campaign typically lasted around six to eight weeks, which made it a great opportunity to do something good and tap into everyone's competitive nature in the process. I am proud to say that my area led the company in the total funds raised for the last five consecutive years before I retired. Our success came because of our great people and two core actions on my part: First, I set a goal prior to the campaign that was attainable yet very aggressive; and second, I measured and communicated the results every single week. (Or actually Bonnie, my great assistant, did.) I recognized the top performers and encouraged those who were lagging. In the end, our team was the best in the company and raised millions of dollars for children's hospitals around the country. Challenge your team with high expectations, and you will be amazed at what they can accomplish.

So what does *good* really look like? The only consistent accurate answer I have ever been able to come up with is that *good* has many definitions. Being that my wife and I spent the majority of my career moving around the country,

15 times in all, we have found ourselves in the situation of shopping for a home on a few different occasions. So many times I would find the perfect house and later learn that it was only perfect in my eyes – or vice versa. Eventually, we learned to find a home that suited us both and was the best choice, one we never regretted. We are all different in our perception of the acceptable, the good, or the great. Caroline and I have been married for 30 years and know each other inside and out, yet we still find that our perceptions of things can be different. How much more is this difference magnified in the workplace?

As part of my job at Walmart, I would spend time each week traveling to stores across the country and evaluating the operational standards and other elements of store operations. I always insisted any time a visitor spent time in a store that they provide a rating for the visit – below standard, standard, or above standard. Why? Because it provides an ongoing calibration of what is expected versus what is actually being done. On occasion, I would visit a store where the conditions needed improving. After touring the facility with the manager, I would meet with the entire management team and ask a simple question of the entire group: How would you rate your store today? After having them write down an answer, we would go around the group and find that almost every person had a different answer. At that point, we would talk about the importance of the management team spending more time discussing expectations and improving daily communications regarding those standards. A few months later I would return to the store to find major improvement. Take the time to ask questions of your teams and listen to their observations and input. Try this exercise with the people you lead. You will be amazed at the variability that often exists in the organizational environment. By closing the gaps in the perception of what is expected, great improvements in standards and consistency of any business can be achieved.

Consistency is a key imperative when considering maintaining high expectations for your overall organization or team. Have you ever felt that the expectations of you or your team were different than those placed on one of your peers? Most of us have experienced this occurrence at some point in our careers. How did it make you feel? I am sure you answered "not very good." Pay attention to that feeling and response so that you ensure you never put your team in that situation. Expectations must be fair and consistent. That does not mean that you cannot expect more from those with higher degrees of experience than those who are new to their roles. The manner in which you establish and communicate what is expected is very important. Talk to your team. Be transparent and let team members know why variances exist if that is the case. Make sure variances can be justified and explained, or do not let them exist. Nothing demotivates a team more than seeing a leader or supervisor justify poor performance or standards in one area only to turn and criticize the same performance in another area. Leaders who practice this approach are unstable and will never gain the respect from or bring out the best in their people.

It is important to remember that expectations cannot be established and forgotten. Conditions change, people change, and situations fluctuate based on numerous factors. I believe that on an annual or quarterly basis, expectations should be discussed among teams and ideas flushed out to understand what has been accomplished and what is possible. Discussions regarding possible roadblocks to achieving goals and standards should be transparent and realized so that strategies and contingency plans can be put in place to mitigate risks. For those who are willing to invest time in the process of setting expectations, quality and high levels of consistent performance against those expectations are often observed. Have you ever worked in an environment where the strategy, priority, or expectation seemed to change almost on a weekly basis? How did that make you feel? Again, frustrated I presume. Remember that feeling and avoid ever putting your team in that predicament. And old proverb says, "A lack of planning on your part does not translate into an emergency on my part." The response most people will have to unorganized, rapidly changing expectations and priorities is to not take them very seriously. Most people will eventually stop reacting to your direction in a timely manner if they know you can't keep up with what you asked them to do the prior week. Be thoughtful in your expectations. Never try to focus on so many things at once that nothing will end up getting accomplished. Keep your message simple, clear, and on point. Differentiate between annual expectations and weekly or monthly tasks that are part of the job. Make sure the weekly and monthly tasks align and support your annual objectives and expectations. Put your energy into the desired long-term result and the parameters the team must operate within. Challenge your people to figure out the best way to achieve those results. Collaboration between the leader and the team is important and will help your people to understand what you are asking of team members and why it is important to the overall goals of the organization.

As it relates to people and expectations, let's discuss the

difference between being committed and being compliant. First, let's look at how each term is defined. Commitment is defined by Merriam-Webster as "a promise to be loyal to someone or something." Merriam–Webster defines compliance as "the act or process of complying to a desire, demand, proposal, or regimen or to coercion or conformity in fulfilling official requirements." I think we would all agree that when people are committed to a cause, great things can happen. Commitment is not a natural response but an earned response as a byproduct of trust. You, as the leader, must inspire your people to understand that they are a part of an overall mission and that you believe in their abilities to do great things. You must instill a sense of trust in them, and they must believe they can trust you in order to be highly committed to their jobs. Commitment is ongoing, from the heart, accompanied with a caring attitude, and runs deeply within the individual, affecting almost all of their actions and responses. People who are committed are the last to quit, the first to speak up when there is a problem, and usually the ones that are bringing forth possible solutions. If you are in a leadership role of any kind, you should continually consider the level of commitment you are observing from your team. If people are simply complying with the minimums required in the job, look in the mirror and realize that you are most likely the problem. Change your approach, go back to chapter one, and make sure you have done a good job of establishing relationship with your people first. Then begin to build upon that foundation one person or group at a time until you are confident your team is committed and aligned behind what you are asking them to do.

So what about compliance? Is there a place for it in the

organizational environment? Absolutely. But compliance is a matter of action, not one of heart. Commitment comes from having a purpose and understanding of why you want me to do what you want me to do. Compliance should be observed only as it relates to ethical behavior, regulatory situations, legal matters, and laws that your business must abide by in order to exist. The problem comes in when leaders take short cuts, try to lead by their titles alone, never get to know their teams, and then wonder why people respond with an attitude of complying versus a commitment to contribute. If you are trying to run your business on a daily basis through the existence of a compliant environment to your direction, you are likely a struggling leader for whom people do not enjoy working. I comply because I have to; it is transactional, non-negotiable, not requiring any thought or consideration. I commit because I believe in you and in the company vision, because I understand the role I play and I know that it matters what I do, and because I know there is reward for me as an individual if I am committed and contribute value to our overall desired result.

The biggest challenge most leaders have when it comes to expectations is the follow through and execution of what was communicated. How many times have you been in a meeting where the leader covers the new plan or expectations for the following year and everyone nods in agreement, and then at the next meeting the same plan is covered again because it was not executed? In most cases, there is a simple reason for lack of execution – poor communication beyond the first level. Setting clear and effective expectations includes the interpretation and cascading of the message to those on the front line.

Everyone on the team must understand the role he or she plays and how it ties to the greater desired result or purpose.

Let's think about this example and how it relates to the sports setting. As we discussed in Chapter 1, relationship with your team must be established first, so you can ensure you have the right people in the right place on the team. Assuming that has been accomplished, if a coach tells a football team at the beginning of the season that the expectation for the team is to win the national championship – and that is the extent of the conversation – it is highly unlikely the team will win very many games. To have a chance at a championship, the expectation must be set at the team level but also at all 11 positions on the field. Each player must understand what *good* and *great* looks like in his position and embrace the realization that if each player is the best at his job, the team collectively will be very successful.

Now think about your organization. If you are reading this book, I assume you have a team of people that report to you and, likely, levels of people that report to them throughout your organization. Communicating expectations to the direct reports is easy; the cascading effect is the challenge. How well do the people on the front line of your business really understand your expectations? Are they committed, or are they simply complying with what they are told? Is your message and that of the company reaching them? Let me offer you a challenge to try an exercise that I tried several years ago. It was eye opening to say the least. At the time, I was a regional vice president in charge of about 100 store locations. From time to time while traveling on the road, I would invite a group of local assistant managers to come to the hotel conference room where I was staying. We would order pizza and spend a few hours discussing what was on their minds. These meetings were a great opportunity for me to understand what questions and concerns the assistant managers had while also understanding the quality of communication continuity between our first-level management teams and me. At one of these meetings I pulled together about 10 very basic questions that I assumed everyone in our region could easily answer. The questions were directly tied to the focus points and expectations we had covered on numerous occasions with upper management in the region. At the end of the night, I came to the realization that my management team and I had a lot of work to do on our communication continuity. We sat in our meetings and discussed great expectations, plans, and ideas that never made it to the people who matter most. If the assistant managers were not getting the message, what did that mean for the hourly associates who played an even more crucial role in our potential success? I challenge you to sit down unannounced and spend some time with your associates, without any other management present. Ask them about their job functions, why they are important, and what role they play in the overall effort of your organization. You may be surprised at what you hear.

There is a bright side of this example I will share with you. After realizing the communication breakdown in our region, I assembled our management team, and we went to work on changing our approach. Through a revitalized effort to follow through all the way to the front line associates, we began to see improved engagement and results almost immediately. We stopped focusing on 10 or 20 objectives at a time and narrowed it to four or five. We started filtering repeat messages and began to protect the team from confusion by providing a clear and consistent message of what was important and why. Realizing this gap led to more disciplined, store-level shift meetings and facility managers who took ownership of these challenges and began to share them with their teams at every level. It made a big difference in our overall regional results, and the team was recognized corporately that year for its accomplishments. Our people led us to the top of most metrics versus our peers that year. Make sure your expectations, and that of your organization are reaching everyone on your team. It is the key to successful execution.

Chapter Two
Reflections

- What percent of the people on your current team would you classify as being committed versus being compliant?
- What can you do differently as a leader to increase the level of committed team members?
- Are the majority of your people contributing with an equal amount of effort toward the established expectations and objectives? If there are major differences, consider what you will do to address the shortfalls.
- How do you feel about your relationship with your top performers versus those contributing less? Are you investing equally into your team, or is the lack of relationship part of the problem?
- Are new ideas being surfaced to you from the field on a consistent basis? If not, do you need to revisit the expectation regarding open communication and remind your people that you value their input?
- When you consider your expectations of your team, are they high enough? Are they too high? Are you celebrating, recognizing, and appreciating your people when expectations are being met and exceeded?

- Are you being fair and consistent across your organization by expecting the same level of effort from everyone? If your answer is yes, is this the answer your people would give if asked?
- Does everyone on your team understand *why* you are asking him to do *what* you are asking him to do?
- When is the last time you walked the front line of your organization and spent time with the people who directly deal with the customer? Are your expectations reflected in their attitudes, performance, and behavior? If not, where is the message breaking down, and how will you address it?
- Most importantly, does everyone on your team (from your direct reports to those on the front line serving the customer) understand what good looks like as it relates to customer service, productivity, ethical behavior, or other elements of success for your particular field of business?

You can have great relationships
with your people, and everyone can
understand what good looks like. But
remember — if your people are not willing
to align behind these common goals and
objectives, success will not come.

Chapter

3

Alignment

When it comes to aligning people behind a common goal, purpose, or set of expectations, it takes leadership. Individuals in leadership roles often will establish relationships with their people and let them know what is expected and then, because of pressures to get immediate results in the business, start managing everyone's actions and attempting to force compliance. This approach is short lived and does not help to build a long-term, effective team. Alignment takes leadership. In his 2004 book *Ready to Lead?*, Alan Price wrote, "Management is the illusion that we can make an irrational world rational. Management creates a story to make sense of the past and guide our actions in the present. Leadership is the imagination that makes a rational world inspirational. Leadership creates a story of the future that makes our present actions meaningful." Lead your people in the direction you want them to go. It may take slightly longer, but it is worth the wait.

As you are working on aligning your team, you should give attention and observation to each individual as much as possible. It is critical that you ensure you have the right people in the right jobs and functions across your organization. At this point, if you are looking at the group and not the individual people, you may miss out on some important clues regarding adjustments that need to be made. Remember that effective leaders will always be transformational with the people around them. In other words, you should be committed to investing in and helping your people become better performers, better employees, better leaders, better members of the community, and more successful in their overall personal careers. The alternative to being transformational with your people is to be transactional. Transactional relationships are without feeling and have little impact on anyone. You give me a check, and I will complete a task. If people on your team are transactional with you or the company you represent, you need to find out why and work to get each person motivated and committed to change. Transactional settings and relationships seldom foster good results or happy successful people. Montana and Charnov wrote, "Transformational leadership is an inspirational form of leadership that has the power to raise organizational expectations, motivate higher performance, and move the business enterprise to a higher level." Great leaders always invest in the future well-being of their people. At the end of the day, this is the one investment that people will remember you by.

As we continue the discussion about alignment, let's take a moment and reflect upon what we have covered thus far in Chapters 1 and 2. Once you are confident that you have established a strong relationship with your team, you should be able to say without hesitation that you have begun to develop a clear understanding of the role each person should play. A foundation of trust should now be established and re-emphasized at every future opportunity. Expectations now have been vetted and discussed. You have listened. You have looked at and discussed different variations of performance and all agreed on what *good* looks like. Now it is time to begin to align your committed team to the expectations that have been established.

As we move from expectations to alignment, it is important that we put these actions in proper context. For the sake of this approach to building your team, remember that expectations will be either short-term or long-term in nature. It is not just the content that you are aligning with your people; it is a process by which you are establishing a protocol for moving forward. Some expectations that need to be established are timeless – integrity, respect, sense of urgency, work ethic, how to handle questions, problems, or roadblocks, and how to handle concerns or disagreements. Alignment to these expectations, as well as to the process for establishing them going forward, is not all-inclusive. While the rules of engagement listed above (integrity for example) are obviously non-negotiable, very few other expectations should be. What? I should not go out and fire people for not following my directions? That's right; you shouldn't, at least not without listening to them first to understand why they took another route.

One of the mistakes leaders and managers often make is thinking that they are the only ones with the answers. Just because you are convinced that your way is the only way does not make it so. Rarely is the person with the biggest title the one with the best ideas. Let's look at a hypothetical situation involving a young lady with great leadership potential who does not understand this truth. The situation occurs at a supervisor-training seminar for a fast-growing coffee company where the founder places great emphasis on customer and employee interaction. During one afternoon of the session, the field managers are broken into small groups with each leading a tour for other attendees in one of the coffee shop locations. As the group approaches the shop, the supervisor leading the tour begins talking about how *she* developed a plethora of plans to address certain challenges in *her* business. She then pulls out a number of checklists and shows everyone how she uses them to conduct her visits. As hourly employees and customers walk by this young lady, she does not appear to see nor acknowledge them. She is so focused on her checklist and her programs that she has become blinded to the very people these processes are intended to serve. After an hour of hearing about checklists, the remainder of the group asks her to consider a different approach and challenges her with a few questions: Which hand do you use to shake hands with the employees being that your arms are full of binders? At what point do you listen to and observe the customer behavior to see how they are being taken care of? And lastly, when do you plan on listening to the concerns of the management team, the employees, and the customers to see how they may need your help? While this new leader means well, her approach and actions demonstrate a top-down, you-know-nothing-I-know-everything attitude toward her team. I am not saying that an occasional checklist is not necessary, but they should be used sparingly so that the leader can stay engaged in listening, observing, and learning from the people he or she is responsible for leading. Checklists should never become a substitute for leadership. This young leader decides to adjust her approach and ends up being very successful and effective in her role.

I spent over 26 years of my management career touring facilities and learning from the people around me. I learned because I asked lots of questions. I learned because I listened. Sam Walton understood the value of asking questions and listening to his people. As a young assistant manager, I observed him doing so, and it never left me. While I only toured a store with Mr. Sam on a few occasions, he made an impression on me that stuck with me for the rest of my career. As Mr. Sam walked a store, he shook hands and often hugged customers and associates. He got down on one knee in meetings and asked the people direct questions. I witnessed him on more than one occasion pulling a manager to the front of the meeting and asking the people, "So how is John treating you guys?" Talk about pressure! As long as John was doing a good job, it was a good moment. He never stopped asking customers questions either: "How are we taking care of you on the front end? How is our inventory? How are our prices and our assortment? Did you find everything you were looking for? What would you like to see us carry that we currently do not have?" Mr. Sam wanted to know the answers to these questions, but most of all, he wanted the people around him, all of the people, to know he valued their opinions.

We are talking about alignment and how we as servant leaders must approach this important action if we want people to respond in the right way. Asking questions, listening, agreeing upon an approach, and making people feel great about taking it. Mr. Sam knew the value of people and how to align them behind a common expectation. He built the company we all know as Walmart today. The power of his servant leadership style and approach speaks for itself.

There is one other personal story that I must share that involved Mr. Sam. There was a small store in the company that had gotten off to a slow start. It was about a year old when Mr. Sam flew in unannounced for a visit. After walking the store with the manager for about 45 minutes, Mr. Sam apparently realized there were problems. He invited all of the department managers (and no one else) to join him at the steakhouse across the street for lunch. How that must have felt watching about 35 of your associates walking across the parking lot to go to lunch with Sam Walton – I can only imagine. During times such as this, a leader must come to grips with the way he or she has treated people along the way. The store manager had issues, and Sam knew it. After about two hours at the steak house, Mr. Sam left to go back to Bentonville, and the department managers returned to work. A week or so later, the store manager was removed, and the following month I was given the store as my first store manager assignment. To say the least, I was very kind to the department managers! Seriously, these people took me in and helped to set me on a path of successful leadership. I still stay in touch with many of these associates, and I appreciate every one of them. Alignment – it is not about forcing people to do what you say. Rather, it is about teaching, motivating, training, and developing in them the skills and the commitment level to complete the mission at hand.

As you enter the season of alignment with your people and your team, some "rules of engagement" should be established. Aligning with the agreed-upon approach or standard takes time, but it cannot become a lifetime journey. If an individual is at point A and the expectation is point D, talk with him or her about incremental goals and expectations and agree upon the progress that needs to be made and in what timeframe. Have patience! This is much easier said than done, but some things do take time. The late Dr. William Bridges has written many great books on the importance of transition, which occurs between the old way of doing things and the new approach. I highly suggest that you add the book *Managing Transitions: Making the Most of Change* to your personal library. I keep a copy on my desk and often reference it for personal and business situations of change. Realize that your people will be experiencing change and transition as you walk through the five steps we are discussing in this book. Talk to them about that change and monitor how well they are aligning to the agreed-upon expectations set for your team. Ask questions and listen to what your people are telling you. As Dr. Bridges wrote, "People who are sure they have the answers stop asking questions. And people who stop asking questions never challenge the status quo. Without such challenges, an organization can drift slowly into deep trouble before it gets a clear signal that something is wrong." The key is for your expectations to become their expectations. In order for this to occur, a great deal of back-and-forth communication must take place.

Have you ever attended a conference call or meeting where an individual gave the group direction and took no personal ownership? Maybe they said something like, "We need to accomplish this by next month with no exceptions because that is what my boss said we must do." Never blame the direction on your boss or anyone else. If you don't believe in the direction and cannot claim it as your own, go talk to your boss and work it out. You need to take personal ownership of whatever you ask of your team. If team members do not see your commitment and passion, they will not have it either. In this same regard, how do you ensure that your team is taking ownership of the direction and expectations you have agreed upon? How can you make sure members embrace alignment and begin to adjust their thinking and actions to align with you and the rest of your team? You have to communicate. You have to follow up. You have to observe and trust but verify often during this stage. You must create an environment where your people know they can push back and ask questions without consequences.

In addition, you have to make sure you are giving attention to everyone involved in the team, not just those who appear to be your best performers at this point. I like what Coach Tony Dungy's father often stated to him as recorded in Dungy's 2007 memoir *Quiet Strength*: "If you're going to be a good teacher, you can't just teach the A students. A good teacher is one who helps everybody earn an A." The perception or reality of favoritism will work against everything else you do to build your team. Make sure you invest in everyone in your organization, not just a select few that you or someone else in the company wants to see move forward.

Let me share with you two trains of thought that have served me well over my years of building teams and working with people. The first is trust but verify (made famous by President Ronald Reagan). Especially during the phase of aligning your team, you must frequently show up at various times and in various places to see what is happening. Be careful not to make it a negative experience at this point but a positive and teaching one instead. In *My Personal Best* (his 2004 memoir), basketball coach John Wooden credited a saying to Abraham Lincoln: "There is nothing stronger than gentleness." You do not have to threaten people to align them. The great leaders throughout history were those who inspired others to greatness versus coercing them. Remember also to be consistent across your organization during this phase. If you show favoritism by going one place unannounced and the following week make your itinerary known, you can easily cause people to begin to question your motive. During these trust-but-verify visits, if things are going well, make a big deal about it and celebrate with recognition. Your people need to know that you are willing to recognize and appreciate their contributions on a consistent basis. As stated so well in the book *Encouraging the Heart* by James Kouzes and Barry Posner, "By lifting the spirits of people [through recognition and celebration], we heighten awareness of organization expectations and humanize values and standards such that we motivate at a deep and enduring level. But even more, public recognition serves as a valuable educational mechanism demonstrating company values and encouraging others to duplicate actions they see rewarded." Always take the time to appreciate your team on every possible occasion. The investment here will have big returns down the road. On the other hand, if things are not progressing as agreed upon, ask questions and try to help get people back on track.

Pay attention both to the individuals who are excelling in this stage and to those who are making no progress. Seek to understand the root cause of the lack of progress. At this point, you have a good relationship with the person and have calibrated what is expected from them, so if progress is not being made, you must seek to understand why. In some cases, it is training. In other situations, it may be that despite your best intentions, you have the individual in the wrong job. While it is not quite time to move them, you should take note of what you observe during the alignment stage, so at the appropriate time, you can make a change.

There is another reason that some people will fail to align with you and the rest of the team: They make a conscious choice not to do so. These individuals may be capable and smart and have great resumes, but if they are not willing to align with you and your team, you have to begin considering other options for them. I have been in this situation several times throughout my career, where despite major efforts to maintain a good relationship and numerous discussions on expectations, some people just will not become part of the team. In Chapter 4, we will discuss how to deal with such situations.

The other approach I would share with you is what I refer to as silent non-compliance. Silent non-compliance occurs when a person agrees to take a certain approach or action up front but then never delivers, discusses roadblocks with you, or suggests a better course of action. Let me encourage you to use this terminology and approach with your team, especially when establishing expectations around alignment and execution. Your responsibility as the leader is to maintain an environment where your people are comfortable telling you if they have better ideas. The salute-and-execute approach is for the military, not for the organizational business environment. While you may be accurate most of the time, there will be occasions where your people have better ideas than you do. Have you created an environment of trust to the point that your team feels comfortable pushing back and telling you why it should not follow a particular directive you have given? When is the last time someone on your team did so? How did you respond? Try telling your team that it always has two options and only two options when it comes to how it responds to your directives. Option one is to make it happen as communicated. If there are no questions or concerns, that means everyone is in agreement and good to go. Or option two is to voice concerns and discuss a better way to accomplish the objective. Taking this approach with your people will ensure you maintain open lines of communication while also improving your team's ability to execute given objectives. This approach will also serve as a means to continually reinforce your relationship with it as a leader who can be trusted and is willing to listen to others. If your people never offer you other options or ideas when discussing a given course of action or objective, take the time to go back and figure out why. Remember that your success is dependent on the success of your people. When people salute and execute, they are complying. When people think and reason and are given ownership in the plan of action, they are committed, and success is imminent.

As we continue to consider the phase of alignment, it is also important that the leader observes those who are beginning to excel ahead of the rest of the group. Who are the early adopters setting the pace for everyone else? Be sure you spend time with this group as well, not just those who are slow to the party. I have learned more over the years from the early adopters on my team than I have from anyone else. As we get into Chapter 4 on making adjustments, we will talk more about how to utilize these individuals to benefit the rest of the team. When you think of alignment, think in terms of individuals, not groups or teams. Remember that we are in the process of building a team; we are not there yet. Think of aligning your people on the team as positioning them for the future, for their future success as well as that of the team. In his 1999 book *The Heart of a Leader*, Ken Blanchard stated the following related to aligning your team: "In business, communicating performance objectives—giving people the final exam questions ahead of time—is the perfect way to ensure that everyone is working from the same sheet of music and headed in the right direction." The alignment stage of building a great team is critical. You can have great relationships with your people, and everyone can understand what good looks like. But remember – if your people are not willing to align behind these common goals and objectives, success will not come.

As Mr. Sam walked a store, he shook hands and often hugged customers and associates. He got down on one knee in meetings and asked the people direct questions.

Chapter Three
Reflections

- Do you have a structure in place in your organization that provides one-on-one support, mentoring, training, and other resources to your people to assist them in aligning to the new expectations?
- Are you leading versus managing your people into alignment and helping them to transform into better performers in the process?
- Are you being fair and equitable with where you are devoting your time and attention and avoiding the perception of favoritism?
- Are you inspiring your people to be great through your personal demonstration of commitment, passion, and enthusiasm?
- Are you asking enough questions and listening more than you are talking on your calls, during your travels, and in your meetings, so you can better understand what your people need, what they are thinking, and how they are feeling about your leadership?
- Are you reinforcing why the expectations are important, the role each individual plays in the team's success, and how each priority is part of the greater vision of the organization, business segment, or company?

- Are you being sensitive to the fact that the people on your team are having to transition from one way of doing things to another? Are you being supportive and patient enough in the process?
- Are top performers being recognized, and are those struggling getting the support and help they need?
- As you spend time with your people during the alignment stage, are you starting to see a pattern of behavior in some individuals where they are simply choosing not to participate? Make note of these behaviors and keep working closely with these people. Sometimes the people who require the most attention to get them to align to the expectations will end up being your top performers. Other times, you have to find them another place to find success besides on your team.
- Are you spending enough time in the trust-but-verify mode? What are you seeing? Are you avoiding the temptation to respond with negativity and criticism and instead offering support and training resources? Accountability will come at a later time, but right now you must help everyone to align with the agreed-upon expectations.

As a leader, it is your job to understand where everyone fits and do whatever it takes to help get them in that position. Leaders who avoid the sometimes-uncomfortable process of making these changes quickly lose the respect of the overall team. Do not be that leader. Be willing to make adjustments in your business organization, but do it the right way.

Chapter 4

Adjustment

Let's take a moment and review what we have discussed in the first three chapters. It is important to remember that each of the five phases covered in this book build upon one another. I call the book *Relationship First* because it is the foundation for everything else we do regarding motivating people, fostering trust, and building a great team. To complement the relationships, we discussed the importance of setting clear expectations with a major emphasis on defining what *good* looks like. Then we moved into a season of alignment where we discussed the need to support, observe, trust but verify, and identify your top and bottom performers.

So to start off Chapter 4, let me first say that many leaders and managers struggle with the adjustment phase of building a great team. Some, in fact, avoid this phase altogether. You most likely have observed situations where adjustments needed to happen within a particular team or organization but never did. The result is often unhappy people, dysfunctional work environments, a lack of teamwork, bitterness, frustration, and most damaging, a lack of respect and trust for the leader of it all. In addition, the maximum performance of the organization and the people involved can never be realized when people are in the wrong roles. As a leader, it is your job to understand where everyone fits and do whatever it takes to help get them in that position. Leaders who avoid the sometimes-uncomfortable process of making these changes quickly lose the respect of the overall team. Do not be that leader. Be willing to make adjustments in your business organization, but do it the right way.

Let me share an example with you of a simple adjustment that I observed early in my career. I was sent to a new store as an assistant manager to help with set-up and grand opening preparations. I had been involved in the hiring from day one and helped to place all of the associates into the various positions around the store. A few weeks into the set up, we began to realize where we had made good decisions on the majority of the placements and where we had obviously placed the wrong person in the given position. One particular associate had been placed in apparel to run a department. She was struggling with the responsibility and could not keep up with the demands of the job. She was unhappy, frustrated, and would have quit soon if the manager had not realized what was happening. While we were all ready to let her go, the manager decided to move her to another position in the store and give her another try. While she could not handle multi-tasking and running a department, she did have other attributes that were of great value. This associate had a voice that was amazing. The manager put her in charge of the phone system, and for the next 20 years or so, that is where she built her career with the company. She was happy, the management team was happy, and most importantly, the customers were happy. How many times have we looked at someone who is failing in a particular role, hourly or management, and simply given up on him or her without a second thought? When it comes to building a great team, you will have to make adjustments, adjustments that affect individual people within the organization, and you have to make these adjustments for the right reasons.

While your first intent should always be to find each person a place where he or she can be successful, at times this position will be outside of the company. As I heard a friend of mine tell a very disruptive ex-employee one time, "You may be happening, but you're not happening here." Sometimes you have to be willing to sit down with a member of your team and wish him or her well in future success, but acknowledge that success is not here and not now. You have to make the tough calls, but with this overall approach of relationship first, you will be amazed how much easier these decisions become when you have built a relationship, established clear expectations, and done all that you can to help the person align with the rest of the team.

There are times and situations where you may observe changes occurring within an organization or team that simply do not make sense. As I mentioned previously, when adjustments are made, they should be made for the right reasons. Leaders will often take over a new team or make changes in an existing team simply to prove to everyone around them that they have the power to do so. This approach is guaranteed to cause that type of leader to ultimately fail and is also likely to hurt individuals within your organization and the performance of the overall group. We have all worked with people in our organizations who may not have been our favorites but were excellent at what they contributed. Take the high road when building your team. Be aware of the decisions you make and ask yourself often what your motives are in making shifts or people changes on the team. If people are moved or not given an opportunity for any reason other than their performance, ability, or behavior, it should raise questions.

Many organizations today have allowed favoritism to creep into the decision-making process regarding people. When leaders do not consider past and current performance as it relates to promotions and future moves, those leaders are most often guilty of favoritism. Don't allow yourself ever to make changes for the wrong reasons. Those leaders are short lived and do not have the respect of those around them. When favoritism exists, you will begin to see such decisions made higher and higher within the organization and less and less at the level it should be – with the team leader. Let us all remind ourselves that as leaders, we have a major responsibility to the people we lead. When changes occur that are driven by us, it affects people's lives in a major way. This is easy to forget when you are being pressured to go against your conscience to satisfy a particular individual, or if you are being pressured to attain better results. If changes need to take place, and often they do, just make sure you can look at yourself in the mirror at night and feel comfortable with the motives and reasoning behind the choices you have made. If you do not feel good about the changes you are being directed to make, talk to someone higher up about it. They likely are not aware of what is occurring at your level. This gut-check will help you to be the great leader you are capable of being, and your people will honor, respect, and trust you for caring about and standing up for their best interests.

So now that we are clear on making needed adjustments and making them for the right reasons, let's discuss why I consider the adjustment phase of building a team so critical. There are many reasons, but the most compelling is the need to protect the standard. I, along with most of you, have worked on teams that were dysfunctional. Everyone on the team knew it was dysfunctional except for the person in charge. Those closest to the leader or person in charge will usually choose to put on blinders and act as though everything is okay. Others on the team begin to have private discussions asking questions as to why the team continues to struggle in the current state and why the leader will not step up and address the challenges. For fear of retaliation or a negative response, most people simply agree to keep rowing and ignoring the hole in the bottom of the boat. As the water level rises and everyone begins to get wet, the leader just keeps pressing forward wondering why the team is not producing. Eventually, the boat sinks and the leader blames the waves while the hole in the boat was never addressed. In some organizations where favoritism exists, the poor leader is simply given a new boat with a new team to sink. In these types of situations, either the leader or key members of the team were not doing their parts or would create ongoing distractions for everyone else in order to keep their attention away from the obvious weakness at the top. At this point, you may be saying that no team can be expected to be perfect, and I could not agree with you more. I am not talking about being perfect but rather being properly positioned. If you can get your team members even 90 percent properly aligned in the positions where they need to be, amazing results will come. When the right people are in the right roles, the team overall can achieve extraordinary results. When people are put in positions they are not qualified for or capable of handling, bad things will happen, or it will take years for someone to learn to function at an average level in a position that needs an immediate contributor.

In most cases, you will have numerous opportunities to build new teams as your career progresses. My wife and I moved 15 times throughout my retail career, and every move meant taking on a new team and driving a higher level of performance. Every situation presented a different set of challenges, a different group of individuals, and a potential great reward. Some positions on your team can be considered developmental, and other roles require someone to hit the ground running. In today's fast moving society, it is critical for you to know the difference. At one point in my career, I ran into a situation that required a change. I had just taken over an existing team that was fairly strong with only a few exceptions. One of the area managers in a particular market was really struggling. He had been in his market for over five years and still had major challenges. I sat down with him and asked how he felt about his stores to understand if we were on the same page with our expectations. He replied and shared with me that at some point soon he would get the stores on the right track. I could not help but wonder, if he had been there for five years and still had not attained a successful level of performance, what made him or me think he was capable of doing so. A few months later, this individual decided he was burned out and needed a change. He chose a new career and found success once again. The point here is simple: Putting an organization or a team on the right track is great, but you cannot take a lifetime to do it.

As a leader, always insist on having the autonomy to build your team. Others will seek to take control of these decisions, and when this occurs, push back. If you are the one who will be held responsible for the results, you should be given a major seat at the table when it comes to placing your team members in the right roles and positions. If your talent decisions are being micromanaged and made for you, it is the likely reason for the misplacements in the first place. Many of you may have seen the movie *Miracle* about the 1980 U.S. Olympic hockey team. I love the film and have discussed it with my team on several occasions as a leadership lesson on building a championship team. In a scene near the beginning of the movie, Coach Herb Brooks is in the process of choosing his players. A committee is pulled together with the mission of approving all of Herb's decisions and each person he wants to put on the team. Herb quickly has enough of the micromanaging and tells the commissioner that he has chosen his team and refuses to take part in the bureaucratic process. With great hesitation and frustration, the commissioner supports Coach Brooks and allows him the right to choose his team. As you may know, the commission never regretted this decision, and the team eventually defied all odds and beat the Soviets to win a gold medal. If Coach Brooks lost all of his games, his decision-making ability would have surely come into question. This is important for you as a leader to remember: You deserve the right to chose your team, but you will also assume responsibility for ensuring your team wins gold. Take the time to make great choices when deciding who will play each position. It takes much longer to deal with the consequences of a bad people decision than it does on the front side to make a good one. Making bad decisions today will result in having to make more and more adjustments in your team tomorrow.

When you do make adjustments within your organization, make sure you put people you trust in the key positions. Make sure you are fully willing to empower the people surrounding you to do their jobs, make decisions, and run their teams autonomously. If leaders are not empowered to make decisions that affect their organizations on a daily basis, they will become frustrated and dependent on you and others to make decisions for them. When trust and empowerment are not present, centralized decision making usually is. Too much centralized decision-making slows progress in the field and quickly turns into bureaucracy. Bureaucracy can paralyze an organization quickly and must be frequently identified and eliminated.

One could easily conclude that the opposite of a bureaucratic environment is one with a strong presence of trust and empowerment. I really appreciate the definition of trust by Angelo Kinicki and Robert Kreitner in their 2009 book *Organizational Behavior: Key Concepts, Skills & Best Practices*, which described trust as "reciprocal faith in others' intentions and behavior." Being trusted and empowered to make people decisions within your team is important. If the right people decisions are not made on the front side, you are simply creating more adjustments that will ultimately have to be made at some point in the future. When I would take over a new team, I often challenged everyone on the team to ensure that from that day forward we only make great people decisions. It really is one of the critical keys to building and maintaining a sustainable and successful team. Take the needed time to make these decisions and do your homework, but do not take forever. You may have observed situations where indecisiveness and doubt from others resulted in critical openings being left unfilled for months on end. This is not a good scenario and the results of such procrastination will cause great delays in the overall team progress. The leader of the team is like the rudder of a big ship. The rudder may not be the power plant, but it is a guide to keep the ship and everyone on it headed in the right direction.

If you find yourself in a situation where your decisions are being micromanaged, you will really enjoy Chapter 6, the perils of micromanagement. I encourage you to be professional, but push back to ensure you have the authority that comes with your level of responsibility. Why do people want to make decisions for you? Because they lack trust. There is likely also a lack of relationship as we have discussed in the previous chapters.

There are two distinctly different approaches that leaders will usually take. As I describe these two styles, ask yourself which one best describes you. The first approach is one of trust that is built on relationship and confidence in the people to do their jobs and make good choices and decisions. If this leader finds that poor decisions are being made on a frequent basis, he will ask questions and demand accountability, but the leader always refuses to micromanage or take away the rightful authority that comes with the given position. The second approach is one of putting people in place but never fully entrusting them with the responsibilities of the job. This leader works endless hours each day, typically making decision after decision that falls well below his pay grade. Why? Good stewardship right? Wrong. Such leaders behave in this manner because they do not trust that anyone on their teams could be as smart as they are. That is a big mistake. This approach also severely limits a leader's ability to think proactively and plan for the future. They are constantly bogged down with the challenges of the moment that they insist on being in the middle of.

Let me give you a simple exercise to conduct as you patronize your favorite places of business. When you are in a place of business, pay attention to the level of empowerment given to those on the front line. If in a department store or grocery store, does every question a cashier encounters require someone else to come over and provide an answer? When shopping in the store, do you hear continual pages for management or supervisors to come running to the rescue? Or is the environment peaceful and orderly with the right people empowered to make immediate decisions on the minimal issues at ground zero with the customers? If the environment is one where no one seems to have the authority to make even the smallest decision on their own, this environment was most likely the result of someone not being willing to make adjustments in their team building process. Do not be that person, and do not make that mistake. The successful leader understands how to put the right people in position and empowers them to do their jobs. In the end, the customer wins, and so does the business. So insist on maintaining the authority you deserve, to make decisions in your space in the organization. If your supervisor does not display a sense of trust in you, ask him or her about it.

Successful leaders and organizations will go to great

lengths to ensure people have the tools they need to do their jobs. If you do not feel comfortable empowering those around you today with these tools, one of two adjustments needs to be made: Either you need to let go of the control you have over your people and start trusting them, or you need to make the needed adjustments on your team so that you put people you can trust in place. Whatever you do, do not settle into a management style of micromanaging your people. It will only result in failure for you and frustration for them. In his 2005 book *Great Motivation Secrets of Great Leaders*, John Baldoni wrote, "Leadership is a journey, a process of moving from one place to another. Sometimes it is easy; most often it is hard and demanding." It will take managerial courage for you to make the needed adjustments along your journey of building a great team.

I encourage you not to settle for average. Once you have made the investment of establishing relationships with your people, worked closely with them on establishing expectations, and allowed them the time and support to align, you are fully justified in making the needed adjustments in your team line up. You are almost to the last and final phase of building a championship team. Make sure you take whatever time is needed to work through the adjustments, and then let's proceed!

Chapter Four
Reflections

- Have you identified the people adjustments that need to be made in your organization?
- Are you prepared and confident in making these adjustments?
- Are you sure that your motives are in check when considering the justifications for the moves you have identified?
- Have you identified options for those affected by the moves you need to make? While some will be outside of the company, remember that some individuals simply need to be given an opportunity to be successful in a different role within the organization.

- Have you taken the time to make sure there is no favoritism present in your decision-making logic?
- Do you have the autonomy to make the decisions you need to make regarding your team? If not, have you pushed back on someone higher in your organization to express your concerns?
- When it comes to the people you are making adjustments with, can you honestly say that you have made the investment of building relationships, discussing expectations, and providing resources and sufficient time for them to get on board? If so, it sounds like you are justified in proceeding forward with your moves. Good job!

Remember that if you build the right team, you can be confident that the individuals are capable of great things. It is your job to bring it out of them by providing an environment of encouragement, trust, optimism, and most importantly, confidence in their abilities to succeed.

Chapter 5

Fine-Tuning

As I stated earlier, not many leaders take the time or make the investment to bring their teams to the fine-tuning stage, but for those that do, there are great rewards. In their 2006 book *212 The Extra Degree*, Sam Parker and Mac Anderson wrote: "Sometimes you'll have immediate exponential results and sometimes you'll realize the benefits of your extra effort much farther down the road. Regardless, in many cases, it may only be that one extra push that gets you ten times the results you were attempting to originally obtain." To begin fine-tuning your team, a firm foundation of trust must first exist among the key players and you the leader. At this point in the team's development, no question should remain as to what good looks like. With the team fully aligned, now it is time to start talking about what defines *great*. As the leader, you should feel confident that you have the right people in the right place, and now you are ready to go beyond the status quo. Fine-tuning a team has a great deal to do with the leader and his or her ability to shift into thinking and leading at a new level. After all, you have done a great deal of work to get your team to this level, and now it is time to see what they are capable of.

We as leaders often have a hard time letting go of authority and decision-making. As your team becomes more mature, let them make more decisions. Increase the level of trust and empowerment you demonstrate to them. This will help them to grow both professionally and personally in the level of confidence they display. When they ask you what to do, ask them what they believe is the best course of action. Remember – great leadership is not defined by how many people obey your commands. Great leadership leaves behind a legacy of empowerment and trust in others that enables them to excel and to be the best they can be. The fine-tuning stage of building a great team should also involve activities that help to prepare your people to move from good to great. It is a good time to encourage your people to consider getting involved in some type of academic activity. This could include the pursuit of a bachelor's or master's degree. Many working professionals think it is too late for them to go back to school. I did not start college until I was 45 years old. I completed my master's degree and graduated with honors in February 2015. Going back to school is one of the best decisions I ever made. Your life experience will propel you throughout the journey. As for your team, it may be helpful for members to take specific courses in areas where you want to see them excel. Numerous courses and development activities are available to choose from. Why is it important to continue to push your people and yourself to learn? It improves critical thinking skills and broadens your perspective. When an individual has strong critical thinking skills, they are constantly willing to challenge their perceptions and routines and are willing to consider better alternatives. This is a very important attribute to have when people are being asked to raise the bar from good to great. That is what fine-tuning is all about.

When we think of the word *tuning*, we often think about an automobile or perhaps an instrument. I recently took my wife's car to the dealer to have some work done. It is a newer model vehicle that the mechanic hooks up to a computer, studies for a few minutes, and then tells me what needs to be done in order for the car to run perfectly. Some models refer to this process as a system-check. The output of different components is quickly scanned and measured against an acceptable standard to see what elements of the engine may need adjusting. It would it be nice if we could take this approach with our teams – just plug people into our smart phones and immediately know exactly what adjustments we need to make. Sorry – there is no app for that, at least not yet anyway. Regarding the tuning of an instrument, we are all familiar with the process of tuning the strings of a guitar. Every string is different in the sound it makes due to being smaller or larger in diameter compared to the other strings. Once properly placed on the guitar in the right position, the musician then begins adjusting each string until it is *in tune* with all the others. Once each of the strings is tuned properly, the guitar makes a synchronized sound where all of the strings complement one another. That synchronized sound is what fine-tuning is all about. That is what great teams do. As you think about these two examples, think about your team today. Is it ready to be fine-tuned? Are you ready to let go of another level of responsibility and allow the people around you to pick it up? If not, go back and reinforce the actions in the first four chapters. If you and your team are ready, then let's take the team to a higher level of thinking and performance.

At this stage, let me give you a few things to consider. Going from bad to good is much easier than going from good to great. As I have worked through this process over the years, there is one common question I have often been asked: How long does all of this take? How long should it take to bring my team to the fine-tuning stage where each of us can be the best at what we do? From my experience, it is better to focus on ensuring each phase of this foundation for a great team is properly established and then let it take as long as necessary. I have taken teams to the fine-tuning stage in as little as a year, where other more complex situations took two and a half years. It really depends on the condition of the team at the starting point and the scope and scale of the challenges presented. Some of you reading this book may be shift supervisors who have teams of six people. This entire process could be completed in a matter of months in this case. To the other extreme, if you are the CEO of a large organization, it will likely take longer due to the number of people involved and the various levels of leadership to impact.

If you are like the majority of people in leadership today, there are two strong words of advice I have for you – slow down. Stop focusing so much on quantity and invest more in the quality of your leadership, your decisions, your time, and your routines. You will be surprised at how much more you can accomplish when you are willing to make slight shifts and adjustments in your routine that help you to become more organized and thoughtful in where you spend your time. If you are a micromanager, your day may be consumed making decisions and dealing with problems that are well below your pay grade. Trust your team to do its job and hold team members accountable. In doing so, you are going to have more time to manage the things on your plate that truly need your attention, while at the same time developing your people to be great leaders. Fine-tuning is about removing obstacles and roadblocks that are preventing your team from going to the next level. By slowing down your pace a bit and looking for these opportunities, you may be amazed at what you find.

Let me give you an example of how this process may look. In your organization, you likely have some type of meeting cadence where you bring your people together on a monthly or quarterly basis to review performance, discuss plans, and cover new updates and such. Have you ever noticed how the open discussion portion of such meetings is always last on the agenda? I do not know why it is this way, but it seems as though everything that can get in the way of protecting this time will do so. Other presentations will either run long throughout the day, or someone will have to leave earlier than planned to catch a flight, and so on. Maybe the open discussion time should be moved to the first thing on the agenda on day one of your meeting. Maybe you should figure out how to incorporate feedback and discussion sessions within each portion of your agenda as opposed to having it separated. Anyway, make this time important. You need to hear what your people have to say. If you invest in this time, it can really propel the fine-tuning process forward. Remember that fine-tuning is not about status quo; it is about becoming great.

To be great, you have to dig deeper and be more determined than ever to find areas and strategies that will deliver these types of results. A great approach to use is to ask the team what obstacles exist today that you can control. Take the time to put the current communication cadence, weekly meeting agenda, and number of emails being sent, all on the table for examination. Remember – we are on a journey to go from good to great. By examining these routines and such, we are not saying they are wrong; we just want to look for every opportunity to be better. Fine-tuning your team is about taking the time to look for the little things that can be improved upon that will make a big difference. This should include looking at your team as a whole, as well as investing some time with each individual.

As you consider the fine-tuning process at the individual level, always start with a good look in the mirror. Change is not always easy. Some may view personal ongoing development as an admission of weakness. The truth is that leaders who continually embrace change are the ones who excel above the rest. These are the leaders who are left standing when all of the others are long gone. Never get so stuck in a routine that you cannot change the way you think. The world around us is changing at a rapid pace. This ongoing change is affecting the way people view their careers and jobs, the way the consumer views their expectations of where to spend their money, and the way leaders must lead. If you settle into one way of doing things for too long, you could quickly find your team left behind. As the leader, keep in mind that you are the one who sets the standard. You are the one who defines good and great. You must keep raising the bar and never let your team settle into a place of complacency when it is producing average results.

Let me share a story with you about the power of raising expectations. Many years ago, I had a particular facility in my area of responsibility that continued to struggle getting out of the status quo rut. The manager of the facility was a great guy, everyone enjoyed working with him, and he had a great deal of respect for his customers and associates. The challenge for this manager was taking his team to the next level of performance. When he had taken over the facility a few years earlier, it was in very bad shape. He and his team had achieved a level of average performance fairly consistently and had become satisfied with their accomplishment. As I stated earlier, it is much easier to go from bad to good than it is to go from good to great. After months of challenging this manager to no avail to raise his expectations and that of his team, I realized we were making little progress and needed something more to get his attention. While meeting with him in his office on one particular visit, I asked him to bring me a permanent magic marker. Very puzzled by this request, he reluctantly did so. After closing the door to his office, I took the marker and drew a straight line mid way across the back of the door. He almost passed out. Next to the line, I wrote the word "average." Then I reached as high as I could to the top of the door, drew another line, and next to it I wrote the word "great." Now, I am not recommending you make drawing on the doors of your workplace a common occurrence, but I must tell you it was pretty effective. After I completed my simple work of art on his office door, we sat and talked about the gap in his expectations that was demonstrated by the space between the two lines. For this particular manager, this was the visual he needed in order to begin to change. Over the next year, he led his team to great. Every visit from that point forward displayed progress on his road to fine-tuning his team, and in doing so it began to perform at a new level. If you want to lead your team to accomplishing great things, you must take the time to invest in it on a consistent basis. When you fine-tune your team and identify root causes of stagnant growth or improvement, you can address those issues and position your business to move to the next level.

Fine-tuning a team is a leadership function. It is important to realize some of the common mental roadblocks that prevent you as the leader from challenging your team to perform at a higher level. This is a time to look deep into the mirror and be willing to face some of your own leadership behaviors that may be preventing your team from breaking out into the extraordinary realm of performance. Why is the mirror so important? Because the higher your title, the more frequently people will simply agree with you on the surface, even if they think your approach is extremely off base. According to David Dotlich and Peter Cairo in the 2003 book *Why CEOs Fail*, "The higher you go in an organization, the less likely other people are to tell you about your failure-producing characteristics." Think about how you view your team and consider if any of these common mistakes apply to you and your team:

- You have an extraordinary team, but individuals are only trusted to perform at an ordinary level with ordinary tasks. Most of you reading this book have worked hard to build great teams that are capable of more than even you realize. Are the goals and objectives you are challenging your people with high enough? Are you allowing your level of trust and empowerment with them to increase?
- Maybe extraordinary results are expected, but only ordinary resources are available. This situation most often occurs in a micromanaging situation. This scenario is very frustrating to everyone on the team.

Remember – if you want team members to go the extra mile, you have to ensure they have the vehicle, empowerment, and resources available to do so. Are you asking them to build a fortress but only giving them resources and empowerment for a small cabin?

- Has the team become so comfortable working together that collaborative disagreement is no longer present? To fine-tune a team, everyone must be willing to discuss new options and new ways of thinking and doing things. In these discussions, it is likely that some will have different ideas regarding what should and should not change. This type of disagreement is healthy and causes the team to press forward continually. If your team members never disagree with one another and believe this type of discussion is no longer needed, they are likely performing at status quo level.
- Are you and the team willing to take risks? Sometimes when a leader is fine-tuning a team and taking it to the level of great, risks are required. Human nature causes our appetite for risk-taking to parallel our confidence level. To relate this to the business environment, if you are asking your team to reach higher and take performance to a new level, team members must feel confident and good about where they are currently performing. Make sure you have built a culture of acknowledgement and appreciation as we have discussed in this book. Sometimes you will have to treat them as the champions you know they can be before they get there. Some of you might be thinking that if your team members are happy with current performance, they might not be motivated to do more. But they will if you use their accomplishments to build confidence and momentum for what is next.

One of the great benefits of fine-tuning a team and raising your expectations for performance is the effect it will have on many of your team members. One of the teams I led in my career needed a confidence boost at one point in order to get members to think about their business performance at a higher level. To help stimulate their thinking, I developed a training plan that we referred to as chief executive officer or CEO training. These 15 market leaders had proven they knew how to perform at a good level but needed a shift in their thinking in order to lead their teams to great. I challenged them throughout the year, as well as in quarterly meetings, to think about their business units as a CEO thinks about his or her company. Many of these managers were running units the size of small companies, so this approach really hit home. In the end, their performance increased, and collectively they led the company in most metrics for the following two years. After completing the CEO training, one of the individuals received a promotion to vice president and moved to another state to take on a new role. Before she left, she thanked me for preparing her for the new role. She said that she felt totally prepared because I had been treating her like a vice president all year, even though at that time she did not see it coming. This was one of the most rewarding things anyone ever said to me. To effectively fine-tune your team, you must see members at a higher level than they often see themselves. This is really important. You must sometimes believe for them what is possible and convey that to them in your communications, your meetings, and in your expectations. In my experience with different leaders over the years, there have been those who continually caused me to do more than I ever thought possible, and those who seemed to encourage me, through their actions and attitudes, to remain average.

Be the type of leader who sees what your team is capable of and make that your focus. Continually treat team members as Super Bowl Champions, even if they have not quite made it there yet. Displaying confidence in your people is a powerful thing. If they know you believe in their abilities to achieve something greater, something greater will usually be the result. If you are one of those leaders who tells your team to get to the Super Bowl and then celebrate, well, good luck with that approach. In my experience, this type of leader only produces perpetual frustration with his or her team. Remember that if you build the right team, you can be confident that the individuals are capable of great things. It is your job to bring it out of them by providing an environment of encouragement, trust, optimism, and most importantly, confidence in their abilities to succeed.

Chapter Five
Reflections

- Do you have a mirror, and are you looking in it often enough?
- Is your team now functioning consistently at a good level, demonstrating that it is ready to pursue great?
- Have you identified areas of responsibility where you can increase the level of trust and empowerment given to your team members? Are you ready to do so?
- Have the big challenges and adjustments previously identified been addressed, and is the morale and engagement level high among your team members?
- Is there a sense of stability among the team's routines, and is everyone on the team functioning collaboratively as one unit?
- Have you let your team know that you are proud of each member and are confident in its ability to go from good to great and achieve even greater results than are presently being produced?

- Are you providing ongoing appreciation and confidence in team members' abilities to perform? Are they fully engaged and ready to raise the bar?
- Are you personally spending time now on problems and challenges that are within your pay band?
- If you answered yes to all of these questions, then you and your team are ready to start fine-tuning and moving your performance and results into an exponential level.
- If you answered no to any of these questions, I suggest you spend some additional time in the first four chapters before proceeding.
- Remember – not many leaders are willing to take their teams to the fine-tuning stage. By following the cadence described in these five chapters, I am confident that you will set your team apart as an example for others to follow. You will have long-lasting results and people who are super-engaged in their roles and responsibilities.

Micromanaging is the enemy of creativity and personal development. When a leader empowers his or her team, it sends a strong message of trust. When people are trusted, they develop the courage to make decisions and go above and beyond what is required.

Chapter

6

The Perils of Micromanaging

Sometimes the best way to understand the right way is first to understand the alternative. If a leader does not take the time to build a team through the *Relationship First* servant leader approach, he will often resort to micromanaging the actions of the individuals around him in an effort to progress and seek to get things done. This is a short-term attempt to lead people and rarely has a positive ending. Have you ever observed a new leader arriving on the scene, usually saying the right things up front, and then quickly giving into the temptation to micromanage the people around him? There is a better way – by establishing relationship as the foundation of your leadership approach and building a team that will have positive impacts on everyone involved. The challenge that many organizations are faced with today is to achieve a healthy balance between leveraging efficiencies and lowering costs throughout the company, while at the same time empowering their people to have the ability to make decisions at a local level.

Even in 1992, it appears that Mr. Sam was thinking about the future, the emerging global economy and the importance of empowerment and decision-making at ground zero. He wrote in his memoir, "In the global economy, successful business is going to do just what Walmart is always trying to do: give more and more responsibility for making decisions to the people who are actually on the firing line, those who deal with the customers every day." Mr. Sam was a visionary and knew the value of empowerment and trust. It is pretty amazing that his words are as relevant today as they were then.

Micromanaging is a very short-term approach to leading people. Have you ever worked for someone who had this style of leadership? While it takes more time, attention, and commitment to build a team through relationship, it is definitely worth going through the process. It is important that we discuss the meaning of micromanaging for purposes of this discussion. There is a fine line between good stewardship and micromanaging. Any effective leader will occasionally dive into the details of a particular situation or segment of the business to trust but verify or to learn more first-hand knowledge on the details involved. This occasional intervention is very effective and demonstrates the willingness to learn new things as well as to follow up on what is expected. However, when a leader consistently questions team members and refrains from delegating the proper level of authority the individuals need to effectively do their jobs, that is micromanaging. This style of management demonstrates a total lack of trust on the part of the manager. When a leader feels that he or she must approve or make every decision, no matter how small within their given area of responsibility, it is actually a sign of insecurity on the part of the leader. If a leader is confident in their authority and in the people they have placed on their team, they will trust and empower team members to make the decisions they need to make to do their jobs. People want to know their leadership trusts them. Of course, there is a timeframe where an individual may need to have a mentor or close supervision during training, but if you put someone in a role to do a job, you must quickly back away and give her an opportunity to make an impact. Holding on to decisions at a high level in an organization is not only damaging and discouraging to the people below, but also very time consuming for the person doing the micromanaging.

Let me encourage you to conduct a quick exercise. Take a few minutes and write down every decision you made in the last two weeks. Then go back and think through each one individually. Ask yourself if each decision should have been made at your level or at a level reporting to you. How long did you sit on the situation before providing the answers? If you are a micromanager, it is likely that you take too long to make decisions because you have time-management issues. In other words, there are so many of the wrong things on your plate, you can't keep up with all of it, which is causing you to exist in a reactive state of mind for 90 percent of the time. If you have made so many decisions in the last two weeks that you cannot remember them all, that might be a sign that you are micromanaging your people.

Leaders need to put the right people in the right jobs around them and build strong teams founded on relationship and trust. Leaders need to keep a healthy balance of thinking about the future and the needs of the business and consumer and not remain bogged down with decisions that should be left three pay levels down. When a leader micromanages, he typically lives in the moment. Often times, so many situations will be making a demand on the leader's attention that only the urgent requests get attention. Managing the decisions of your people is often an alternative to developing talent. You should think twice before putting people in positions based on their "runway" or "long-term" potential alone. In today's fast-moving business environment, people have to start contributing quickly and, therefore, must be trusted and empowered to make decisions that affect their jobs. You may have put a person in a job for the wrong reason or without properly ensuring he was capable and ready for the particular responsibility. Instead of dealing with the root cause of the problem as we discussed in Chapter 4, you allowed the person to remain while making all of the important decisions for him. This is not a good approach and cannot be maintained for very long. If you have a trust issue with someone on your team, address the situation with a more permanent solution.

When people are not empowered to make timely and appropriate decisions, they often become paralyzed in the moment and can become extremely frustrated with the person creating the micromanaging and bureaucracy. Over time, the employees affected can lose concern for the problem, eventually giving up and believing that if no one above them cares about the problem they shouldn't either.

This can severely damage relationships with customers and their trust with the company. Be courageous and invest the authority and empowerment you have been given to your people. If you have a confidence deficit, it is likely a problem that everyone else can see but you. Be confident in who you are and in the fact that someone believed in you, or they would not have put you in your role. Do not go to work fearing failure, or you will never be able to empower others with the autonomy and trust they need and deserve.

Leaders must have the courage to experience failures along the way. Without occasional test-and-learn situations, your organization can become stagnant, stuck in a rut and out of touch with the customer. If people are not occasionally failing, they are afraid to try new things and explore new ideas. Micromanaging is the enemy of creativity and personal development. When a leader empowers his or her team, it sends a strong message of trust. When people are trusted, they develop the courage to make decisions and go above and beyond what is required. When people have courage, they are more likely to demonstrate a high level of commitment to results and to the success of the company.

Let me share an example with you of the damage micromanaging can do to a team. A new executive joins an automotive company at a very high level. He is excited and cannot wait to get started on his new assignment. Several months into the job, he still has not made time to get to know his team and puts it off until he gets caught up. A year later, he finds himself working very long hours each day, seven days a week, trying to keep up with the demands of the job. His team members do not trust the executive because they hardly know anything about him. He continues to tell everyone that as soon as he gets time, he will sit down and get to know everyone better. It never happens. For fear of making a mistake, this leader decided he would be better off making the final approval for almost every decision his team needed to make. Open positions that should have only required his direct reports to sign off were stacking up and not being filled because he insisted on reviewing them, even though he did not have time to do so. What really did not make sense about this situation was the fact that he did not know any of the people who were up for the jobs. The people who worked for this leader were at their wits end as he seldom returned phone calls or emails due to being so busy. Every time they did talk to him, he would postpone the decision pending more details and information they had to spend time pulling together. When a leader takes this approach with people, eventually the team members grows weary in feeling that they have to prove everything to the one decision maker in the group before they can proceed. Needless to say, this leader ultimately failed and left the company after only a few years. Be a leader who is willing to let your people fail once in a while. Allow them to run their business units, and in doing so you will also allow them to win, to learn, to grow, and to enjoy working for you and the company.

I think we have all been guilty of micromanaging at some point in our careers. The good thing about having a great relationship with your people is that they will tell you when you are getting too far away from your proper level of responsibility, as long as you create an environment for them to do so. I have been amazed on so many occasions when the people I supervised came up with solutions and ideas far beyond that which I had previously considered. When I trusted them, challenged them, and allowed them to take ownership of their responsibilities, the results almost always exceeded what was expected. Mr. Sam was a believer in fostering decision-making at the field level and understood the danger of a company becoming too centralized in its decision-making. He wrote, "At our size today, there's all sorts of pressure to regiment and standardize and operate as a centrally driven chain, where everything is decided on high and passed down to the stores. In a system like that, there's absolutely no room for creativity, no place for the entrepreneur or promoter. Man, I'd hate to work at a place like that, and I worry every single day about Walmart becoming that way." Some of you might read this quote from Mr. Sam and argue that things are different today than they were 22 years ago. Today, there are tougher regulations, compliance issues, legal requirements, and other factors that make companies put stringent controls in place in order to minimize corporate exposure and risk. You are partially correct. Some things are different, but we also must realize that when it comes to human behavior, some things never change. This is the important point that many in leadership overlook. The human spirit is still driven by a need to be appreciated, trusted, valued, and engaged. People have an inherit need to be a part of something that they consider of value and purpose. If their ability to create, think, innovate, and imagine are all taken away from them, they become numb to their jobs, which become nothing more than transactional relationships. Good leadership is all about discerning those things that can be left to the people to decide versus the issues that cannot. When micromanaging is present, it typically invades even the small decisions that should be left to the control of those in direct contact with the situation.

So why do so many leaders struggle with letting go of control? Sometimes it's ego. Other times it's inexperience or wanting to be in total control. And then there are situations where the leader simply does not trust his or her team. Kinicki and Roberts wrote, "Egos influence how we treat others as well as our receptiveness to being influenced by others." Regardless of the reason, let me encourage you to avoid making decisions for your people at all cost. You will be amazed at what a little bit of trust and empowerment will produce.

The challenge that many organizations are faced with today is to achieve a healthy balance between leveraging efficiencies and lowering costs throughout the company, while at the same time empowering their people to have the ability to make decisions at a local level.

Chapter Six
Reflections

- When you examine the recent decisions you have made in your leadership role, were they truly situations that required your involvement?
- Do you find yourself struggling to answer emails or phone calls in a timely manner? Do you occasionally become guilty of prolonged decision making? If so, you may need to consider empowering your people with a greater level of authority.
- Do you really trust your team and direct reports? If so, do your actions align with your words?
- When times get tough and the pressure increases to produce better results, do you start making all of the decisions for your people, or do you release their creativity even further to help surface potential solutions?

- Do your people trust you? If you hesitate on your answer, there might be an opportunity for you to consider behavior changes to make sure.
- Do you provide your team members the opportunity to be creative and innovative within their space, or do you simply manage their level of execution? Both are important.
- How would you describe your ego? Would your people around you have the same response?

Be a leader your people can respect, trust, and count on to bring out the best in each of them. If you put Relationship First, people will climb mountains for you and the company and in doing so will achieve great personal success as well.

Chapter 7

Bringing it all together

Relationship, expectations, alignment, adjustment, and fine-tuning – follow these consecutive steps to build a championship team that you can be very proud of. This approach is not the only way to build a great team, but it is a proven and very effective means of embracing success for you and your people. This approach and this entire book are written from the perspective of servant leadership. Servant leadership is not a term that one hears discussed very often in today's business environment. That is the very reason I was inspired to write this book – to remind anyone in leadership that the way to the human will is through the heart. When Sam Walton came into my store in the late 1980s, his first mission was not to evaluate the store's operation, nor was it to see if the facility was clean or well merchandised. Sam Walton's first priority was to talk to the people and listen to what they had to say. Mr. Sam invited my two fellow assistant managers and me to sit down in the snack bar and have a cup of coffee. He pulled out his yellow note pad and began to scribble out our names and where we were from. He asked us questions about our town, our store, and our customers. He listened to our thoughts and wanted to know what he could do to help us take better care of our associates and our customers. While Sam's actions may seem simple to most, they were life changing to me as a 21-year-old assistant manager. Sam had a way of making anyone feel comfortable in his presence, and he inspired them by believing they could do anything they set their minds to. He kept leadership simple – listen, encourage, support, inspire, challenge, and appreciate. Sam Walton was the definition of servant leadership. As we got up from the snack bar that day, we toured the store with Mr. Sam. As he walked the aisles, he thanked us for many things and challenged us on a few as well. When he left, I remember thinking that was how I wanted people to feel about my leadership. Mr. Sam set a great example for us all. While many things have changed since the days that Mr. Sam walked his stores, there are many things that have *not* changed. People want to know their leaders care about them and their futures. People need to hear hope and confidence from their leadership, along with trust and an ongoing sense of optimism. People will not respond positively to leaders who have ego problems or insist on micromanaging all of their teams' decisions. Remember that the business environment is not the military. In the military, individuals sign up to serve. In the business world, people have needs that are to be served by their leadership. People want you to listen to what they have to say.

When writing an evaluation for one of your direct reports, do you take the time to call some of the people who serve under that person to hear their perspective and input? Most of the time this never happens, which makes one wonder how the supervisor truly knows what to write in the evaluation. It is important that you know how the people feel about that individual's leadership, and the only way to understand this is to hear it from a few of them. Doing otherwise means that you value your opinion and no one else's. Great leaders will embrace and acknowledge the reality of where their people are but never limit the possibilities of where they can go and what they can achieve. Great leaders will press through the favoritism and noise to truly understand the heart of each person they are leading.

Be a leader your people can respect, trust, and count on to bring out the best in each of them. If you put *Relationship First*, people will climb mountains for you and the company and, in doing so, will achieve great personal success as well. If you resolve to make all the decisions and limit the choices made in your organization to your perspective, your success will be short lived. Invest in others, be a servant leader, treat people with respect and appreciation, ask lots of questions, and be a great listener.

I wish you great success in your leadership journey. May you leave behind a legacy that is defined by the success of the people who were proud to call you their leader.

References

Baldoni, John. *Great Motivation Secrets of Great Leaders*. New York: McGraw-Hill Publishing, 2005.

Blanchard, Ken. *The Heart of a Leader*. Tulsa, Oklahoma: Honor Books, 1999.

Bridges, William. *Managing Transitions*. 2nd ed. Cambridge, Massachusetts: Da Capo Press, 2003.

Ciardi, Mark and Gordon Gray, producers, and Gavin O'Connor, director. *Miracle*. [Motion picture]. USA: Buena Vista Pictures Distribution, 2004.

Conlow, Richard. *Excellence in Supervision*. Fairport, New York: Axzo Press, 2001.

Dotlich, David and Peter Cairo. *Why CEO's Fail*. San Francisco: Jossey-Bass, Wiley imprint, 2003.

Dungy, Tony and Nathan Whitaker. *Quiet Strength*. Carol Stream, Illinois: Tyndale House Publishers, 2004.

Gostick, Adrian and Chester Elton. *The Carrot Principle*. New York: Free Press – A division of Simon & Schuster, Inc., 2007.

Kinicki, Angelo and Robert Kreitner. *Organizational Behavior: Key Concepts, Skills & Best Practices*. New York: McGraw-Hill Irwin, 2009.

Kouzes, James and Barry Posner. *Encouraging the Heart*. San Francisco: Jossey-Bass, 1999.

Merriam-Webster online dictionary. http://www.merriam-webster.com/dictionary/

Montana, Patrick J. and Bruce H. Charnov. *Management*. Hauppauge, New York: Barron's Educational Series, 2008.

Northouse, Peter. *Leadership: Theory and Practice*. Thousand Oaks, California: SAGE Publications, 2010.

Parker, Sam and Mac Anderson. *212 The Extra Degree*. Aurora, Illinois: Simple Truths, 2006.

Price, Alan. *Ready to Lead?* San Francisco: John Wiley & Sons, 2004.

Soderquist, Don. *The Wal-Mart Way*. Nashville, Tennessee: Thomas Nelson, Inc., 2005.

Walton, Sam and John Huey. *Sam Walton: Made in America*. New York: Bantam Doubleday Dell Publishing Group, Inc., 1992.

Wooden, John and Steve Jamison. *My Personal Best*. New York: McGraw-Hill, 2004.

Young, Stephen. *Micro Messaging: Why Great Leadership is Beyond Words*. New York: McGraw-Hill Companies, 2007.

About the Author

Coming from humble beginnings, Henry Jordan learned the value of hard work and motivation at a very early age. Henry joined Walmart in 1985 as a stock associate and moved through the ranks of operations for the next twenty-eight years, working as a department manager, assistant manager, store manager, and district manager. After serving as the director of operations for the Neighborhood Markets, he was promoted to regional vice president and then to senior divisional vice president over the Eastern Seaboard Division, one of only twelve divisions within the company at that time.

Always a leader, Henry's countless contributions include successfully opening the first forty Supercenters in the state of California and the first Supercenters in Washington, D.C. He was also instrumental in the development and success of Walmart's Neighborhood Markets, serving as the first director of operations in the format's early stages.

During his successful Walmart career, Henry served as a true culture ambassador for the company and has always been a consummate student of retail and leadership. He is a recipient of the Sam H. Walton Hero Award given in recognition for his servant leadership and for teaching a young man how to read.

Believing in supporting his local community, Henry had the privilege to serve on the board of many organizations as well. Realizing the importance of being involved in the markets where he operated, Henry has always sought out community opportunities to serve others.

Today, Henry enjoys sharing his passion for teaching and inspiring the next generation of leaders to be their best. Henry is an avid dog lover and enjoys spending time with his rambunctious Jack Russell terrier named Chance. In 2012, Henry coordinated a year-long, pet-adoption initiative that helped save the lives of more than one thousand animals from surrounding pet shelters in the Eastern Seaboard. He and his wife of 30 years, Caroline, share a dedication to their faith, a love of the great outdoors, and an adventurous spirit of travel. Henry earned his bachelor's degree in 2013 and his master's degree in management in 2015.

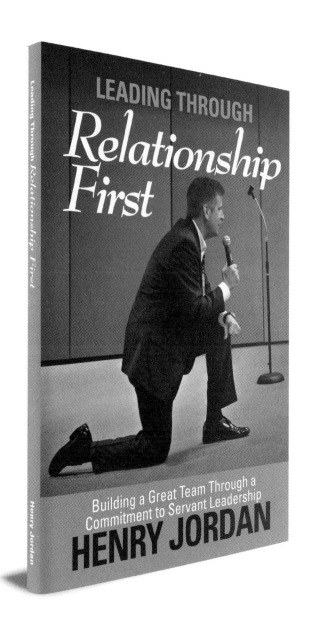

To order additional copies or learn more about
Henry Jordan, please visit
www.henryjordanleadership.com.